Who am I

and where am I going from here?

James Lewis

Published by Purpose Publishing
1503 Main Street #168 ✱ Grandview, Missouri
www.purposepublishing.com

ISBN: 978-0982837-962

Copyright © 2013, James Lewis

Cover design by: Thaddeus Jordan
Editing by: Brenda Cotton

Printed in the United States of America

This book, or parts thereof, may not be reproduced, stored in a retrieval system, or transmitted in any form or by means – electronic, mechanical, photocopy, recording, or any other without the prior permission of the publisher.

This book is available at quantity discounts for bulk purchases. Inquiries may be addressed to:
www.FRGODMINISTRIES.com

Email us at: ministerjames.frgod@gmail.com

Scripture used in this book are noted from the KJV of the Bible

DEDICATION

This book is dedicated to all of the people whose lives seem to drift without direction due to divorce, separation or death. Grace will show you who you are and your destined position in Him.

Introduction
    Who Am I and Where Am I Going From Here?   11

Chapter 1
    Who Is In Charge?   19

Chapter 2
    Fathers: God's Representative to the Family   29

Chapter 3
    The Seed Releaser and Initiator   39

Chapter 4
    Daddy, the Trainer   49

Chapter 5
    Affection Creates Destiny   77

Chapter 6
    Fatherhood: A Priestly Servant   87

Chapter 7
    Mom, the Warrior   115

Chapter 8
    Mothers: Christ's Model to the Family   125

ACKNOWLEDGEMENTS

A special thanks to my spouse's parents, Swinton and Maggie Haynes. Without their connection with the Lord Jesus, my wife would not be the blessed wife and mother that she is.

To my parents, Loran and Lois Lewis. I am godly proud to be called your son. Thanks so very much for the instruction and guidance through life's challenges and for introducing me to Jesus Christ.

To our children, Quan (Danielle), Shanita (Alvin), Joey, Krystal (Alex), Rachel (Earl), and Jamie. Thank you for allowing yourselves to be fathered and mothered by us and instructed to grow under our guidance. Also for challenging me to be a father, and a servant to you all.

Thanks to three special people, Ms. Linda Fillyaw, Mr. Steven Redick and Mr. Frank Pink for your commitment and connection with our family.

To my best, best, best friend, who pressed me and encouraged me to write, my spouse Rae. Our love is never ending and I love you for your consistency, your diligence and love for God and our family.

Thanks to my spiritual fathers, Rev. John T. Olds, Pastor Horace Sheppard Jr., Pastor David Cotto, Apostle Keith Wesley Sr., and my father, both naturally and spiritually, Loran C. Lewis, Sr.

To my spiritual mothers, Sis. AnnaMae Olds, Rev. Linda Sheppard, Rev. Tina Cotto, Pastor Lisa Wesley and my mother, both naturally and spiritually, Minister Lois Lewis, Sr.

Thanks to my siblings: Loretta (Arthur), Pastor Lois June (James), Loran Carl, Leitha, Lydia, Lesley, John (Debra), Altha, Clifton (LaTonya), Jeffrey, Zelma, Alexander and Lee Edward.

Also, thanks to Rae's siblings: Pauline (Max), Edward, Swinton, Jr. (Bernice), Lankford, Elmer (Wanda), Fredrick, Beatrice (Leroy), Gerald (Sherita) and Robert (Leslie).

FOREWORD

It was one day in 1990. I was driving home as usual from work listening to a Christian Radio station. I don't recall what program was on, however, Joni Eareckson Tada was speaking about her life story. She was sharing about how active she had been with various sports such as horseback riding, hiking, and swimming, until the day her world was turned upside down. She had dove into a shallow part of the water at Chesapeake Bay and severely injured herself, becoming paralyzed from her shoulders all the way down to her feet. Her life was forever changed and she became a quadriplegic.

She expressed how she went through depression, anger, suicidal thoughts and doubts about God during her rehabilitation. However, she did not allow her circumstances to overtake or consume her completely. She sought the Lord and He gave her a special talent in painting and writing. Her artwork became a sensation. She has written a best-selling autobiography, obtained numerous awards, honorary doctorate degrees and is an international conference speaker! Mrs. Tada also has a ministry called "Joni and Friends" that is worldwide.

As I listened intently to her story, I began to cry. All I could imagine was a shriveled up body that no one would want to look at and all of the pain, rejection, scorn, and ridicule that she must have felt.

Sound familiar? Jesus, our Lord and Saviour, went through that when He was beaten and nailed to the cross at Calvary. As the tears flowed from my eyes while driving, the Lord spoke to my heart saying, "This is how many of your children, step-children, and adopted children feel." These children have been thrown together by a decision their parents made and now they have to live with that decision and begin to ask, "<u>Who Am I and Where Am I Going From Here</u>?"

As parents, when we don't follow God's standards, our children are forced on a path that they are unfamiliar with, searching for a secure place in life.

I shared with my husband, James, what the Lord had spoken to me and encouraged him to write this book that I believe will bless all the families of the earth.

Pastor Horace Sheppard counseled with our blended family which, I believe, helped us to start down a godly path for the success of our family.

Although, we have hit many bumps along the way, over the years, God has constantly been in the plan and we now have an opportunity to share with other blended families our story.

INTRODUCTION

WHO AM I AND WHERE AM I GOING FROM HERE?

In our socio-economic structure, the family is the backbone of our churches, communities, schools and businesses. Everyone that contributes to the strength of these entities were brought (conceived by sex) into this world by a man and a woman, entering them into a family. The structure may be solid, cracked, crumbled or on the verge of demolition, but each child is still identified as a part of a family, whether their parents are known or unknown. Unfortunately, some children are growing up without knowledge of their beginnings or security for their future; they do not know who they are or where they are going. Parents many times, do not know of their heritage, and that is not only speaking of a godly heritage.

Two women and a child (or children) do not constitute a family, nor does two men and children. Although they may be entitled to marry one another one day, since God never ordained or instituted it, neither of these types of relationships are able to properly be acknowledged as a family. They are illegal in the eyes of God. They cannot reproduce another human being because they have the same "plumbing" or sexual organs. These types of relationships are not nuclear nor are they to be considered a blended family, even if it is because of demanded rights, gender problems, illegitimate births or the promotion of alternative lifestyles.

Homosexual or lesbian bonding will never legitimize them to God's purpose of procreation and family.

Also, a man and a woman living together without the marriage contract do not constitute a nuclear or blended family. These positions have weakened the family unit because of the attempt to exclude God's Word of creating one man and one woman to cleave unto each other, becoming one flesh. **"Therefore shall a man leave his father and his mother and shall cleave (commitment unto death) unto his wife: and they shall be one flesh"** (Genesis 2:24). There is a blessing in obeying God's Word - just do it His way.

The commitment to one another, the joy of service and the consummation of intimacy (after marriage), activates the eternal genealogy of the covenant-maker. I believe God established the family first so that we could identify our relationship with Him and His relationship with us. Love, commitment, submission, obedience, faithfulness, trustworthiness and loyalty are some of the principled foundations that we need to experience in order to gain characteristics that exemplify His traits. These character traits help the fruit to grow as we branch off into other human relationships, providing strength to the family. God helps us to identify with a beginning and a future.

We are experiencing character flaws in our leaders because we are not connected to the power source, which is God. Therefore, the symptoms of low morality, divorce, illegitimate births, and abortions are a direct result of a broken relationship with God. We want substance (possessions) over integrity. Before

Introduction

there were governing bodies in the world, church or community, God first gave roles to the man and woman to be fruitful and multiply, imparting hope to the next generation of the will of God. The family is supposed to be protected by the governing bodies that God ordained. Instead, the state government, federal government, and sometimes even the church have worked against the family.

In Matthew 19, the leaders of Israel went to Jesus with questions about divorce and marriage. They wanted to know if it was lawful for a man to put away his wife for anything. It was clear they had no regard for God's future plans for the family. Jesus, Himself said that this was not the way God intended it, even though divorce was allowed. And it was only allowed because of the hardness of their hearts. Does this sound familiar to present day marriages? We want to pass laws that will allow us to do what our hard hearts want. So, when our hearts are hardened to the truth then our families suffer, marriages fail, we remarry, and our children become confused and have to adjust to new relationships and new surroundings. Children can even become puzzled about who they are. With the many people that can come in and out of their lives, it can become difficult to know how they fit into the equation of the family body.

You are probably still asking, "What makes up a blended family?" Good question, and I think a brief history of my, or should I say *our* family, should give you a good idea. I'll start with my wife, Rae. As my deceased father-in-law would say, she is Rae Haynes-Redick-Pink-Lewis. She was born to Swinton and Maggie Haynes, the fifth of ten children, seven brothers and two sisters, one of which has passed. She grew up in a Christian home. She has multiple names because I am her third husband. From her first husband a son, Quan, was born. From her second husband a daughter, Rachel, was born. She was at a tender age of 19 when she was first married, then at a riper age of 24 with her second marriage and I received her, in the prime of the harvest season, at 33. However, before her father could put Lewis on the end of her many last names, he passed away in June of 1988, six months before our union on December 31st. I am sad that I never had the opportunity to call him Dad, but I did know him to be a spiritual leader and a father in Christ Jesus; for he was a deacon and a trustee on the board at our local church in Topeka, KS. - Capital City Community Church of God.

    I am the ninth child conceived by Loran and Lois Lewis, Sr. Seven sisters and six brothers are a result of their time together. However, both of my parents, two brothers and two sisters have passed away. I am also from a Christian home.

    Now, I want to explain what I mean by a Christian home. Our parents—both Rae's and mine—taught us to be like Christ; they prayed with us and for us. They took us to "church services" and showed us an example of how to live godly lives. They did not just teach us values, but they lived it. Our fathers were "promise keepers" before the movement came forth. I have been married once before, adopting two of my first wife's children, Shanita and Joey. (My mother felt Joey needed a real name instead of a nickname, so we called him Joseph so that God could take away his reproach and my mother would be pleased. But he is still accustomed to being called Joey and still goes by that name.) Two more children were born to my

Introduction

first union, Krystal and Jamie. So Quan and Rachel are half-brother and sister, Shanita and Joseph are full brother and sister, and Krystal and Jamie are full sisters. However, with my first marriage, two of the former and two of the latter were half brother and half sisters all having the same mother but different fathers. And since God is a God of many chances, He put Rae and I together, giving us another chance after making us complete in Him.

So now Rae is a step-mother to four children and a biological mother to two children. I am a step-adopted father to two children, and biological father to two children. I also adopted Rachel in 1999, so now I am a step-adopted father to her as well. So, to sum it up, there are step-brothers and sisters, half brothers and sisters and full brothers and sisters. God's touch of grace has blended us together. Do you get the picture now?

This, I hope helps you to see God's hope for the family, no matter what you have experienced or are experiencing even right now. Sometimes things get confusing, but you try to make sense of it. It could be an unplanned pregnancy, divorce, remarriage or a first time marriage with a person who has children. Whatever it may be, there is hope from God to blend everything together. So, I hope this book blesses you and yours.

Who Am I and Where Am I Going From Here?

Identify your family's relationships. What areas do you need to leave and decide to cleave unto your mate or your immediate family?

Introduction

How do you see God's grace and the Holy Spirit blending your family together?

_____
_____
_____
_____
_____
_____
_____
_____
_____
_____
_____
_____
_____
_____
_____
_____

CHAPTER 1

WHO IS IN CHARGE?

This has been a popular question for marriages from the beginning of sin. God spoke to Man to leave the tree of the knowledge of good and evil alone, however Man did not listen to God. Instead, he listened to the woman. It was at this moment that he became submissive to the woman, and not to God. Male and female are equal and should work side by side, but positions cannot be switched. God ordained order in the family. **"But I want you to know that the head of every man is Christ, the head of woman is man, and the head of Christ is God"** (1 Corinthians 11:3). Even the changing of laws will not change God's positional purpose for each gender. Nor will He allow the children to take the place of the parents. In our time now, the equality issue is very sensitive since minority groups, women and children's rights groups and homosexuals are fighting to compete with the established power. Submission leaves some, with a bad taste in their mouths. But submission is a sweet word, for without it we would have chaos.

We are submissive to ideas, philosophies, religions, laws and God. Whatever we believe in or however we live, we submit to that authority. In a biological family, it is tough enough to establish leadership because two different backgrounds are merging in an attempt to form one standard for the children. On the inverse, in a blended home, there may be four or more background traits to deal with. I will talk more about this later, but as I stated previously, homosexuals, lesbians, or heterosexual couples that are living together without a marriage license do not constitute a blended family.

There are three important questions in any family. Firstly, "What is my position?" For example, "Am I a father, mother, son or daughter?" Secondly, "What are the roles that go with my position?" And thirdly, "Who gave me this authority?"

Let us look into the first question, "What is my position?"

We were born to be either one of two types of homo sapiens, male or female. We do not choose; the chromosomes chose for us, and God knew which one we would be. Therefore, when we grow up, we remain a male or a female - actually, a physically developed male or female, called a man or woman. If we marry, we remain a male or female, but now we are called a husband or wife. God created the male first, and then he took the female from the male's side, or his rib. (My wife, Rae is my "prime rib!") This is illustrated in Genesis 2:21-22, **"And the LORD God caused a deep sleep to fall upon Adam, and he slept: and he took one of his ribs and closed up the flesh instead thereof; And the rib, which the LORD God had taken from man, made he a woman, and brought her unto the man."**

Secondly, God's divine ordinance was for male and female to reproduce, so Adam and Eve reproduced. Then their children reproduced, and so on and so forth for thousands of generations. We are all equal, however, the woman was taken out of man and shaped by God to help the man to do what God ordered as mentioned in Genesis 2:18, **"And the LORD God said, It is not good that the man should be alone; I will make him an help meet for him"** (Genesis 2:18).

It is important to understand that we are all equal, but not interchangeable. The shape of the body, facial hair, and physical strength normally are the differences. Although there may be some women endowed with excessive hair or strong, muscular bodies, it is not the norm. Some men may look or act feminine, but again, it is not the norm. No matter what they look like with clothes on, it is the way they look without clothes that counts. God's intent is for the man to be the head, to submit to Christ, and to love the woman by sacrificing for her in every way. The woman is to submit to him and his position as the visionary and head of the home. The children are to submit to (honor and obey) their parents, pleasing God. **"Children, obey your parents in all things: for this is well pleasing unto the Lord,"**

The Bible says in Colossians 3:20, we need training to help convey our positions to fulfill our purposes. Men are the head of the home and women are the heart of the home. Young males need to be trained on how to be a good husband and a good leader, while the young females need to know how to be a good wife and heart of the home. We have too many role reversals that confuse our children.

The next question is, "What are the roles that go with my position?"

There is an old saying: "Too many cooks ruin the meal!" In my home, in sports and in work experiences, I have noticed that everyone was not in charge, but everyone had a role to perform. Your position defines your role. The father has the last word in the family because he is the head of his family. He is the director or delegator and the visionary for the home. When the man is either absent from the home or is not in touch with God, then the vision is clouded.

Many times, God directs the mother to give the vision to the children, but usually the mother is to be empowered to help direct the home. She is to complement the director and pass on the vision. The children are to receive this vision and follow it, and then pass it on to the next generation. God said in Exodus 20:6, **"And showing mercy unto thousands of them that love Me and keep My commandments."**

Everyday, the vision needs to be lived before the eyes of our children so they can live it before the eyes of their peers. When the male and female Adam was deceived in the Garden of Eden, God called for the man to answer first. Why is that? The woman was the first to be deceived by the serpent, so why was she not called out first by God to answer for her transgression? This was because God expected the man to stand on the Word that was first given to him, before the woman came on the scene. God gave the male, Adam, the vision and expected him to relay it to his wife. When the female, Eve, refused to listen to the visionary, the male, Adam had a choice to make: either listen to his first instructions from God, or to his wife's instructions, which came from the serpent. He chose to listen to his wife's words and not God's.

This does not mean that husbands should never listen to their wives, but they should weigh their decisions on whether their wife's words would glorify

Who Is In Charge?

God or not. Adam should have interceded for his wife, but he chose to keep silent and spoil the plan of God.

As a man of my home, I would be crazy to stand back and watch someone come in and tell my wife things that are not true. Even though the female sinned first, God chastens by position. The man may have the last word, but he gets the first reprimand because he gave his authority to his wife and the serpent. Spiritually, death came to his household along with shame, guilt, and separation from his Creator and he was expelled from paradise (Eden). **"Therefore the LORD God sent him forth from the garden of Eden, to till the ground from whence he was taken"** (Genesis 3:23).

The last question is the most important one - "Who gave me this authority? "

Your position gives you much authority. The man has the most, and the woman has as much, however the man is held by God as the one most responsible for the outcome of the family. The child has the least authority. For example, a policeman has enough authority to stop traffic, make arrests, and to make the citizens do what he asks. But his jurisdiction only goes so far, whereas the FBI is able to cross state lines when necessary. Even within the police force there is rank and the higher the rank, the more authority the policeman has.

Mothers are like Christ in the home.

I have gotten into several fights growing up because someone talked about my family. It is said, "blood is thicker than water." I exercised my authority to protect my home even though I was not in charge.

I could make sure the outsiders stayed outside, even with their comments.

When we were raising our children, Rae and I would periodically go out together, telling the children not to let certain people in the house. We gave all of them authority, but we would put our eldest son in charge over them. If they did not mind him, they were not minding us. If we allowed people in, it was because we felt we knew them. We gave them authority to use it correctly, but they could have abused it.

God put us in families to learn how authority is to be used properly. However we use this authority, whether right or wrong, we will answer to the One who created us and gave us this authority, so we need to listen to Him and stay in our lane.

Find out what your role is and use the authority that goes with it. Jesus represented the Father; He brought glory to Him. He talked to Him daily and sometimes all night. He wanted to do whatever was asked of Him. Mothers are like Christ in the home. They represent the husband, (Father) communicating with him to bring forth the glory of the father to the children and outsiders. In a blended home, understanding your position and exercising your authority is very important. Children who do not accept one another as brothers and sisters by the marriage covenant will find it hard to accept God and His family (The Church). While the parents are the key to the togetherness, mothers are the mediators that keep the legacy flowing. **"Wisdom has builded her house, she has hewn out her seven pillars"** (Proverbs 9:1).

Who Is In Charge?

Identify who is in charge or has the last word in your home?

Do you feel comfortable being in authority, delegating authority or just not exercising your authority?

Do your children identify their right to protect the family's name or do they let others run down the family?

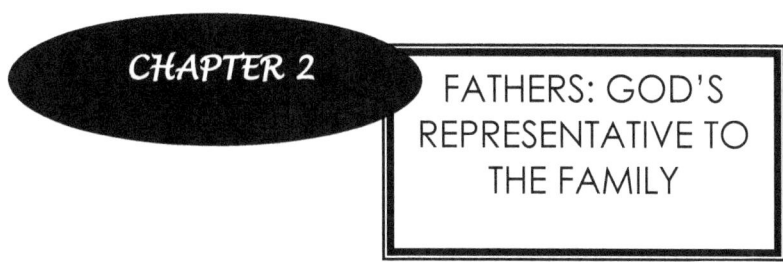

CHAPTER 2
FATHERS: GOD'S REPRESENTATIVE TO THE FAMILY

God instituted marriage before the government or the church, as was explained in the first chapter. In the Garden of Eden, man did not need redemption or laws to govern him; he was in perfect union and harmony with God. He was getting direct commands from his Creator as they had a face-to-face relationship. However, the Creator saw that he did not have another person suitable for him. Since there were other creatures that were suitable for each other, God said it was not good for man to be alone. If you separate that word "alone" it means "all one." There was life in him that needed to be brought out to subdue and occupy the world that was created. Man could not subdue the earth by himself, so He put man to sleep, took one of his ribs and formed it into a woman - a helper, the carrier of his seed, and a companion - to fulfill the purpose of the Creator. Man was first created, and then the woman was created for the man. **"For the man is not of the woman; but the woman of the man"** (I Corinthians 11:8).

God gave man and woman positions while they were alive, which were to harmoniously reproduce offspring similar to them. Man was the person that was the overseer, and protector of the home, the garden. The woman was to submit to his authority, to carry out the task that was given to him, for the man had a direct command from God what to do in the garden.

Simply said, she was to help him complete the task given - nothing more and nothing less.

Although God says that the man is head over the woman, it does not mean to rule or dominate. It is by order of the position given, where man is a covering for her, to protect, guide, love, honor, direct, care for and nurture; to continue the heritage given to him from his Creator. His wife is to be beside him. When a man is successful in fulfilling his position, the woman is comfortable in fulfilling hers. For beside every successful man is a successful woman, helping him in fulfilling God's plan for their home. The two of them were to have dominion over all the beasts, birds, fish and great creatures in the sea. They were never to be in bondage, or addicted, to anything that comes from the earth. They were also to be fruitful and to multiply; reproducing after their kind to subdue the whole earth. **"Then God blessed them, and God said to them. Be fruitful and multiply; fill the earth and subdue it; have dominion over every living thing that moves on the earth"** (Genesis 1:28). No mention of evolution here.

Communication was open; there were no secrets, no hidden agendas, and no shame. But we have an enemy attacking our minds with lies and misconceptions. Satan crafted a plan of getting mankind to think God was not honest or truthful. He convinced them to believe God had a hidden agenda and was restricting them from having all knowledge like God. Satan was an outsider, and many persons on the outside make their way to the inside to get the family twisted. He started with putting doubt in their thought-patterns, making them believe that the head—God—was not being truthful; causing their God-consciousness to be replaced by self-awareness and intellectualism. This is illustrated in Genesis 3:4-5: **"And the serpent said unto the woman, ye shall not surely die: For God doth know that in the day ye eat thereof, then your eyes shall be opened, and ye shall be as gods, knowing good and evil."**

Next, Satan's plan was executed deviously to have the man follow the woman's lead, which was not in line with the Word that was given to them. God is the First and the Last, the Beginning and the Ending, the Author and the Finisher. He is the initiator of order, truth and purpose. Creation was to emulate the Creator, hearkening to His Word. Since they disobeyed, confusion, role reversal, shame, closed mouths, finger pointing, hiding and blaming the Creator and each other, was the result. Instead of accepting fault and placing the responsibility where it belonged (on Satan and themselves), they blamed God.

Something worse happened that we have a tendency to over look. It is that mankind became separated from a relationship with a loving God - the overseer of the family and all other life-functioning organizations - that bring prosperity, purity, peace and righteousness to mankind. Dysfunction in the family began because things now were perverted and distorted from the original blueprint of God. Open communication was gone and unity changed to disunity; they did not trust each other. Jealousy and envy, strife, infidelity and pain became their friends.

But God! He has put his stamp of approval on marriages and families and He is not taking it back. **"Marriage is honorable in all, and the bed is undefiled:**

but whoremongers and adulterers God will judge" (Hebrews 13:4). God will judge all who twist, pervert, distort and discredit marriage. But God's judgment is not to condemn, it is to keep His institution pure and just.

While I was at work many years ago, there were some of my coworkers and most were single, but a few were married. The single men would urge some of the married men to meet them at the bar after work for some drinks. If the married men said they had to check with their wives first, they would get ridiculed. Well, you know what happened next? Many of the married men wanted to prove they were not "whipped", so they conceded and listened to an outside source daring them to prove that they were "the man". But they did not realize those outside voices would not be able to reconcile them with their wives if problems would arise. Although some men were able to work through the miscommunication, some were not able to recover from their poor decisions. Wisdom builds your house, so the principal thing is "beware of the outsiders!"

Since God has put His stamp of approval on the family, each member's relationship must first be vertical with God then horizontal with each other. This means we must have a personal relationship with God, then with each other. Our institutions thrive off of families to keep them going. We even expect our Presidents to be married and to have good family values; unfortunately, some Presidents have not always abided by them. But the expectation is if they are married and already have children that they have raised or are raising, they have experienced what America stands for, "the family." For we believe that

Fathers: God's Representative to the Family

God is about relationships and it starts at home. Even the Church emphasis is a marriage covenant with Christ which is our bridegroom: "**And Jesus said unto them, can the children of the bride chamber mourn, as long as the bridegroom is with them? But the days will come, when the bridegroom shall be taken from them, and then shall be taken from them, and then shall they fast**" (Matthew 9:15).

Colossians 1:17-18

> And He is before all things and in Him all things consist. And He is the head of the body, the Church, who is the beginning, the firstborn from the dead, that in all things He may have the preeminence.

Ephesians 5:23-28

> For the husband is the head of the wife, even as Christ is the head of the Church; and He is the savior of the body. Therefore as the Church is subject unto Christ, so let the wives be to their own husbands in every thing. Husbands, love your wives, even as Christ also loved the Church, and gave Himself for it; That He might sanctify and cleanse it with the washing of water by the word, that He might present it to Himself a glorious Church, not having spot or wrinkle, or any such thing; but that it should be holy and without blemish. So ought men to love their wives as their own bodies. He that loves his wife loves himself.

Who Am I and Where Am I Going From Here?

Jesus Christ is the head of the body, the Church and the symbol for husbands to be shown how to love their wives.

As a man, I am to love my wife as Christ loved the church and to give myself for her. Before a man will have a position in the Church, he must be the husband of one wife and he must rule his house well. Even his children should listen with respect. This does not mean his children must be perfect, but they should hearken to their father's instruction and their father should be able to hear their needs and teach them, not provoking them to anger, but to do good deeds.

Even the media focuses on family values. They may be twisted in their expression or their attack on the family, but they do realize that families are essential to the success of a nation. If there was someone that had done everything in their power to keep you from prospering, it was more than likely you were a threat to them. You either had something they wanted, something they could not have or something they knew would benefit you towards success. So the issues of healthy families or unhealthy families are written about in our newspapers, magazines, in movies, TV sitcoms, documentaries, and discussed on talk shows. It is also being researched, studied, eulogized, revived, criticized, scrutinized and analyzed, but it has not changed the value of the family, nor the impact strong healthy families have on our society.

Now, since families are a central focus of our nation, let us take a look at one of the main positions or roles in it, the father. Since the beginning of time, the father has been the target of destruction, since authority and dominion was given to him over all the earth. His enemies know if the head is destroyed, the rest of the family would be scattered. Usually when the enemy would attack their opposition, they go after the most dangerous position or person that has authority to destroy them. The man (father) is that person and has the position in our families. However, his enemy, if we understand him, is crafty and sly and will not come directly at the fathers, but through indirect avenues that are not expected. He uses subtle manipulation and cunning methods.

In slavery, just the simple changing of a name could change the destiny of a race of people, for the name identifies those of their past and future, where they are from and where they are going. In America, fathers carry the family's name and give the heritage. As I said in the introduction, I adopted three of my children, giving them the last name of my forefathers. They have identified themselves to be Lewis' and their character is shaped by what has shaped me, not innately or by physical traits, but mentally and spiritually.

In the 70's, there were not as many single parent homes, but with the increase of sex outside of marriage, drugs, alcohol, divorce and women's rights, fathers are becoming more and more extinct. Fathers are being castrated by welfare and homosexuality. Crimes committed by men are always a sure way to fatherless families. Satan appears to have the upper hand in his demise of fathers, but God says in the last days He will turn it around: **"And He shall turn the heart of the fathers to the children, and the heart of the children to their fathers, lest I come and smite the earth with a curse"** (Malachi 4:6).

Ask yourself: Am I, as a father, involved with my children and their lives or are they involved in mine? Am I a good, so-so, or a poor representative of God, the Father?

Fathers: God's Representative to the Family

Do I know my children's bent (their personality, tendencies, demeanor, skills, talents)? Do I know if they have received Christ, and their giftedness?

CHAPTER 3

THE SEED RELEASER AND INITIATOR

We label fathers as "deadbeats", "candy dads", "AWOL dads", "abusive", "dictators", "wimps", or "henpecked". And we have lauded them as "hard workers", "leaders", "visionaries", "tender warriors", "loving", and "caring", and I am sure you could think of a lot more names. There have been good movies and bad movies about fathers. There have been movements such as, "Men of Integrity" and "Promise Keepers" to edify all men. Even the "Million Man March", a few years ago, wanted to build up the Black man, to make atonement for the sins done by, and to, us men. However, I must mention that Jesus is the only one that is able to make atonement for the world, (mankind) by the shedding of his blood; for He is the only one able to make all races of men whole and productive. We cannot make atonement for each other or ourselves; and we definitely do not have a Black Messiah or a White Messiah.

Jesus is the Messiah for all who would accept His finished work on Calvary's cross. He showed His work by conquering death forever in His resurrection and passing into the heavens and now He is seated on the right hand of God the Father. "**Seeing then that we have a great high priest, that is passed into the heavens, Jesus the Son of God, let us hold fast our profession**" (Hebrews 4:14). There was none before Him, and there will not be anyone after Him to atone for our sins.

Other movements have been staged to eradicate or redefine fatherhood, such as "gay rights." "Homosexual Day" was placed on Father's Day a number of years ago, and liberal organizations, such as the ACLU (American Civil Liberty Union), are propagating agendas against fathers, trying to undermine God's positioning of men. God's anointed seal of approval on the fathers are unequaled in business, government, or any organization.

A man can be a success at work, in sports (professionally and recreationally) but a failure at home, and God will address the home life first. He requires men to be accountable. After everything is said and done, men want to measure up as either being a good father or to say they were a father figure to someone. In God's Word, He addressed Adam after their disobedience by eating the fruit: **"And the LORD God called unto Adam and said unto him, 'Where art thou?'"** (Genesis 3:9). God wants us to produce good fruit (children) with Him. When a man becomes righteous, (which is in right standing with God) his nature changes, he releases a good seed and his fruit (children) becomes a tree of life to win souls. He will be recompensed (rewarded) in the earth: **"The fruit of the righteous is a tree of life; and he that wins souls is wise. Behold, the righteous shall be recompensed in the earth: much more than the wicked and the sinner"** (Proverbs 11:30-31). Fathers will initiate honest lifestyles for their children knowing that he is kept by the righteous hand of God: **"A righteous man hates lying: but a wicked man is loathsome (acts disgustingly), and comes to shame. Righteousness**

The Seed Releaser and Initiator

keeps him that is upright in the way: but wickedness overthrows the sinner" (Proverbs 13:5-6).

Fathers who will fear (reverence) the Lord, and delight themselves in His commandments, his seed (offspring) shall be mighty and blessed. Also wealth and riches shall be in his house and his righteousness will endure forever:

Psalms 112: 1-2

> *Praise ye the LORD. I will praise the LORD with my whole heart, in the assembly of the upright, and in the congregation. The works of the LORD are great, sought out of all them that have pleasure therein. His work is honorable and glorious: and his righteousness endures forever.*

These are scriptures that speak of God's anointing on a humble, surrendered father. I suggest you read Psalms and Proverbs to gain wisdom and understanding.

Fatherhood is a tough position because of the accountability and responsibility it requires. Fathers cannot afford to neglect their responsibilities with their family; the results have greatly impacted society in a negative way. The non-committed or non-empathetic dad needs to change. There are too many single mothers with fatherless children filling up our cities and rural areas.

It used to be considered the right thing to do, if a man got a woman pregnant, to marry her. The couple faced some tough challenges, but it removed a fatherless label off of the child and the young woman had a personal commitment from the father of their child. Even though they may not have been in love, they committed themselves to each other and worked together in the responsibility of raising their child. They were not selfish and they made a vow before God and man that was not to be broken. **"If a man find a damsel that is a virgin, which is not betrothed, and lay hold on her, and lie with her, and they be found; then the man that lay with her shall give unto the damsel's father fifty shekels of silver, and she shall be his wife; because he has humbled her, he may not put her away all his days"** (Deuteronomy 22:28-29).

Selfishness and pride are the two biggest reasons for a man not providing for the woman they got pregnant and the child they fathered. "It's not mine," "It can't be mine," "It will cramp my style," "I thought you were protected," or "Why did you have to get pregnant anyway?" are some of the common excuses, cover-ups, or smoke screens of a selfish and prideful attitude. Women cannot get pregnant on their own and if she was having sex with someone else, what are you doing having sex with her too? Could it be for selfish reasons? The woman could have been selfish too, but her reasons do not rationalize the man's non-committed and selfish attitude.

I heard a well known family psychologist say, "Men use love to get sex, and women use sex to get love" and it hit me because I was like that, doing things to show I loved my wife to get sex. And the games we play as guys trying to coerce the females into an act of sexual pleasure are for our selfish desires.

I now understand why God says, **run away from fornication; for the sin of fornication is a sin against the body, your own** (1 Corinthians 6:18).

Fathers are the initiators of relationships and they need to know what principles to follow to have wholesome relationships. **"Flee also youthful lusts: but follow righteousness, faith, charity, peace with them that call on the Lord out of a pure heart"** (I Timothy 2:22). If you are single and wanting to have a successful marriage, abstinence is the best and only way to go to prepare for a godly marriage and to fulfill the family covenant. It also is a good shield from sexually transmitted diseases. However, some of us have created this mess and it is not going away.

So men, admit your heart, if it is selfish, prideful or you do not want the responsibility, repent and ask the Lord, Jesus Christ to change your heart. Then God can clean up the mess and turn your family into a blessed one. God made you to release a good seed into the earth to continue His heritage and your children will be His reward.

Ask yourselves these questions: "Do I see myself as a initiator or a victim of circumstance?" "Am I releasing blessings or curses?" "Do I see myself as a blessed man that fears God?" "Why or why not?" "How can I show my wife good loving intentions without her sensing a selfish reason?" "Is there anything hindering my family's success?"

Psalm 128: 1-4

Blessed is everyone that fears the LORD; that walks in his ways. For thou shalt eat the labor of thine hands: happy shalt thou be, and it shall be well with thee. Thy wife shall be as a fruitful vine by the sides of thine house: thy children like olive plants round about thy table. Behold, that thus shall the man be blessed that fears the Lord

The Seed Releaser and Initiator

Am I leading my children by setting the example into their destined place? Am I pointing the way for my children to go?

Who Am I and Where Am I Going From Here?

Do my children the image of the desired result of the seed that I have released and planted?

Am I clear in communicating the desired result?

CHAPTER 4

DADDY, THE TRAINER

Since fathers are the head of their household, he must be alert, knowledgeable, in touch with their children's needs, their personality and their talents. Fathers, keep up with the times that you live in; it could be very detrimental to your child's well-being if you are not carefully paying attention to what they watch and who they spend time with. It could mean their lives. With a blended family, take extra time to spend with each child in getting to know them and their likes and dislikes. In Proverbs 22:6 it reads, **"Train up a child in the way he should go: and when he is old, he will not depart from it."** The way that he should go is actually according to what God has put in the child.

God has a certain purpose planned for each child to fulfill His planned outcome - to produce prosperity for them and their family. As the Dad, you are the trainer and as the trainer, ask yourself, "What am I training my children for?" "Who am I training them to serve?" This reminds me to say, **"Seek first the kingdom of God and His righteousness and all these things will be given to you"** (Matthew 6:33). Everything you have need of will be provided to give to your children. The Word of God is our most precious commodity and children are the ones we pour this treasure into.

For children from broken homes who have been cracked or scratched, it is imperative to first have the damaged parts mended by establishing a working relationship with them. Spending time with each child in your new household lessens the tension. I cannot tell you if it is more important to get to know your stepchild or your natural child, because if you pay attention to one and neglect the other, it will cause many problems. Many times we want to focus on the child we have just come to know and we lose sight of the one we thought we knew. Take a night to just talk to the children, individually, seeing what their interests are.

> *My mother once told me that children see the image of God through their fathers. Now that I am older I believe it even more.*

I made a mistake of not taking the time of doing this with the older three in the early stages of our relationship, but I learned to do it later in their lives. Now, do not get discouraged if this does not work at first. The child may need time to get a feel for you. It is harder to do this with a teenager, but not impossible as they need attention also. The worse thing is to let the child formulate assumptions about you and your feelings toward them. Even if the child does not particularly appreciate you, they will respect you for your persistence. Think if you and your wife just brought your newborn baby home, you would not leave the baby to themselves; you would allow the child to get a feel for you by holding them, talking and playing with them. Use this same principle in getting to know your new family members. Talk about your life before they came into your life. Ask them about their friends, school, habits, hobbies, or whatever. Little people are like big people, they like to talk about themselves and they want to know if you are interested in them.

Daddy, the Trainer

The Greek title for Father is "Pater" and the intimate name in Hebrew is "Abba". Intimacy, fellowship, guidance and security are your tools in building your house so your children will carry it on to their children. **"For as many as are led by the Spirit of God, they are the sons of God. For you have not received the spirit of bondage again to fear; but you have received the Spirit of adoption, whereby we cry, Abba, Father"** (Romans 8:14-15). The Spirit of God leads the sons of God (born-again believers) after they receive the Spirit of adoption (legal acceptance into the family). Therefore, they can now call God, Father. So now since He is their Father he has the authority to train and instruct His children.

My mother once told me that children see the image of God through their fathers. Now that I am older I believe it even more. Sometimes, fathers seem distant from their children and need to have a mediator, which is their mother, to speak and intercede for them. I saw my father as a man of discipline, a worker, someone that was there for support, and to put fear (respect) in my heart. He trained my brothers and I in every aspect in our lives. But early in my life, I needed my mother to help me communicate with my father. I was not as intimate with my father in my teenage years and he was not with me.

Many fathers will carry their sons early in life, showing intimacy to them, but usually when they get to school age they tend to speak to them harder than they should. My youngest son introduced me to the "father-son" hug. He has a personality that is very sociable. Sometimes he drew attention from questionable people at school and usually every other place he went. He challenged me to show him godly, unconditional love. Even though I had to be tough with him, he demanded a tender touch. He was funny and could make you laugh, but he was also sensitive. I was not used to this type of sensitivity; my father was funny but did not teach us to wear our feelings on our sleeves. Even though we were very close, we did not overtly show affection. I only started hugging my father and brothers later in my life. This interaction spread to my oldest son who was more like me. Then this carried over to how I interacted with my sons-in-law and grandsons.

Being a "Daddy" calls for us to use our four tools to demonstrate to new children their usefulness to the family structure. When little girls play house, they bring to life that which is imaginary, using their creativity to make the ideal home what they want it to be when they are grown up. Fathers and mothers have to create an ideal environment to bring purpose and destiny to the lives of their "little pearls". A father's inappropriate touch to their daughters could damage their relationship for life, or a good touch could draw them so close that not even a cute boy would break it up. And be careful not to provoke children to anger with harsh words. My relationship with my daughters and sons was not the best at first because I was too much of a disciplinarian to them and did not give them the good touch, but in their teenage years I worked to keep them close, and my wife helped me understand them.

What traits of God are you displaying to your children? There is a presumed trait of God that is false; this is that He is a God that is ready to punish people. This idea is usually derived from dads that ruled their families with threats and punishments. It may not have been right for the fathers to do that, but that was what they knew. Remembering my mother's aforementioned view on how children see their fathers, we have come to believe that God is like our dads, getting angry over the smallest matters. This may be a bad perception of God and fathers, but it is real in the minds of people. Fathers need to show intimacy to dispel misconceptions, problems, chaotic situations, or anything else to keep the family fellowship on the right track. It is important to understand that for a biological family, even though everyone is different there are similar traits and thought-patterns. On the inverse, in a blended family, everyone is different but the thought-patterns are formulated and shaped by the actions of the parents, not an innate trait.

Intimacy builds relationships. Children feel at ease when they know their father cares for them just as they are, without a performance record. This small beginning of love draws men to be close to their children, fellowshipping at any cost. I have heard many young people claim they wanted to have a child to love them. Many times it is because they did not experience the love with their fathers. Intimacy goes to the person who needs love; security is to be there to give it.

Children are not in the position to be the initiator of love, but the recipient. Children need security and guidance. Love puts those barriers around the family to give your children a healthy growing process. You are not their friend and yet you are to befriend them. You are to know their talents and gifted areas and bring out the best in them. And your love needs to be secured, to take them up and down the highway of life to the different stages of growth until it is time for them to start a family. God became a man to die for us; we are to externally live the gifts He placed in us to give our children sight of this awesome love.

My two sons were on restriction at one time for two months straight. This placed a strain on their outlook of God the Father. I was provoking my children to wrath by piling on one restriction after another. My Father is a gracious one, so He let me know to reprieve them, no matter the severity of the offence. Rae was all for it and you know the boys were too. They did not become good kids, but it did help me to give unmerited favor, which is grace. Children should not have to perform to gain love from their fathers. We, men, are performance-driven. We live by sight, taste, touch, smell and what we hear. Men love to compete and conquer. Unfortunately, we are conquered by the things we involve ourselves in. None of us are exempt from being competitive, for our world is set up to compete whether it be for jobs, sports, honors academically or socially, even for wives.

If we measure our child's success by comparing them to others instead of training them to do their best, then we frustrate them to problems. There will always be someone better, faster and smarter, even if they reach the top, time will tell on them and someone will come around to take over. Grace understands their value as a person to be respected and loved, so men give your children touches of grace.

One touch of grace is acceptance. When your step- or adopted child has berated you and is very disrespectful to your authority as the father, they may tell you that you are not their real father so they do not need to listen to you. Other statements may be, "You do not give me the attention you give to your own children." Or maybe you have heard this one from your own child, "Ever since you married her, you play favorites with her and her children and neglect me." I have heard these remarks and others. It would upset me because it was not my intent to be partial. However, grace sometimes makes it look like a person is getting special treatment, since it is favor and favor is not earned. It is acceptance into the family based upon someone else's actions.

Children do not ask to be in their particular family; it was the actions of a man and a woman, whether sexually or legally through marriage or adoption. God the Father writes, **"To the praise of the glory of His grace, wherein He has made us accepted in the beloved. In whom we have redemption through His blood, the forgiveness of sins, according to the riches of His grace"** (Ephesians 1:6-7). Jesus is His beloved Son that died for us and He accepts the fact that we need Him. Our children need us and we need to give grace. But if you, as a father, have never received grace, it is impossible to give it.

The first thing is to ask Jesus into your heart and accept His redemptive work on the cross for your salvation. If you have done this, you may show grace by being quick to listen, slow to speak and slow to anger. **"Wherefore, my beloved brethren, let every man be swift to hear, slow to speak, slow to wrath. For the wrath of man work not the righteousness of God"** (James 1:19-20).

Seldom take issue with what the child says;

grace discerns the real issue. God the Father sees the big picture and we do not. So our reaction is tainted by our physical senses - what we see, hear and feel.

There are some things to consider when it concerns the feelings of your child. Insecurity is a major consideration, whether it is warranted or not. When a new person enters the family picture, some children may not feel there is enough love to go around. Or, since their old family structure broke up, they may not be sure of this one.

Then there is vengeance. Children who have been hurt, are sometimes defensive and want to do the hurting instead of being hurt. It could be anxiety or the fear of opening up. Nonetheless, they will guard their heart. Animosity, envy and jealousy sometimes arise toward their new siblings as there is now competition for your attention. Too many times we use our position on them which usually does not confront the real issue. "Do it because I am your father," is what we may say. Evaluation of the circumstance and persons involved is necessary. Show your new child they are loved by you and you are genuinely interested in them.

Children naturally feel loyal to their parents. But in a blended home, the thought may be that loyalty is earned. Oftentimes children will feel disloyal to the parent that they are not attached to, and it seems if they have not received love, they will not accept love or give love for fear they have betrayed the other parent. Grace reassures them that everything will be taken care of. It is what children need - a reminder that they do not need to earn love. It also reminds your natural child that you have enough love to give everyone what they need. Grace listens more to their worth than their actions.

God gave us two ears, not to balance out our heads, or to keep our hats from falling over our eyes, but to listen more than we talk. I found out that to put stock on their performance frustrates and confuses them; they cannot figure out what to do. So they work harder and harder to please their parent without building character or they even might just quit, feeling worthless; that they will never be good enough.

This takes us to the next touch of grace, which is compassion. Compassion is to be kindhearted in bad situations, even when you are right or they brought it on themselves after multiple warnings. It is not human to be empathetic or compassionate, but it is godly. To be human is to say "I told you so," or give them a lecture. This may work sometimes, but teaching them with compassion seems to help the youngster accept their responsibilities and the actions of others easier. It helps them focus on what they have done and see that God's love is expressed even when they mess up. God is compassionate!

Fathers, as was stated before, are prone to provoking their children to anger. If not, God would not have written it in His Bible: **"Fathers provoke not your children to anger, lest they be discouraged"** (Colossians 3:21). When a father's expectations are higher than what may be accomplished, they tend to rely on their own strength to be self-reliant and strong. Fathers want that in their children, especially their sons. However, since everyone depends on someone or something, a person can never be completely self-reliant.

Provocation comes when a picture is painted that is a negative indication of the child's success, i.e. if they do not make the grades we expect, get the right job, or make the play on the court or field. The pressure to achieve forces them to have an unattainable standard, all the while restricting them in finding their own niche. Many times, fathers stress that their success comes from their ability to pull themselves up by their own bootstraps. This gives them a false sense of their own security and abilities. Pride is a crack in the steps of the success ladder - step on them and it is a humiliating fall.

God is the one to instill talents in people. Self-motivation, self-esteem and self-reliance only encourages us to not put our trust in the only wholly self-sufficient one, Jehovah God. When a man starts to think he does not need God or anyone else, circumstances come to humble them to get their attention. The same applies for our children.

My definition of compassion is to be aware of a person's faults and shortcomings, then passionately aiding them in a time of need. **"Finally, be ye all of one mind, having compassion one of another, love as brethren, be pitiful, be courteous: Not rendering evil for evil, or railing for railing: but contrariwise blessing; knowing that ye are there unto called, that ye should inherit a blessing"** (I Peter 3:8-9). Jesus had compassion and healed them, fed them, taught them, and delivered them. **"And Jesus, when He came out, saw much people, and was moved with compassion toward them, because they were as sheep not having a shepherd: and He began to teach them many things"** (Mark 6:34). Whatever it took to help man be compassionate, Jesus is the only one to help man to accomplish it. He first shows us compassion and mercy. In Lamentations 3:22-23, it says, **"It is of the LORD's mercies that we are not consumed, because His compassions fail not. They are new every morning; great is thy faithfulness."**

This brings us to the next touch of grace - mercy. I remember one of my sons got in trouble at school. He was in the 5th or 6th grade and he was in the principal's office, which I worked for at that time. I talked to him, telling him not to get in any more trouble or he would receive a good spanking for this problem. Well, within the hour, he was in trouble again and they called me for a meeting. I was furious and my pride was hurt; he was not listening, he did not take heed, and now I felt, he was challenging me, bringing our name to shame. I told him very angrily that he was in for it. When he got home, he told his sisters to tell me he ran away. After picking up Rae from work, I arrived home to hear of this alleged escape. I did not believe them so I looked around the house, but could not find him. You see, he had pulled this stunt before. Well it was getting time for us to go to prayer meeting, so I felt I needed to look in his room again. I was about to look under his bed when the Spirit of the Lord told me he was there, but to leave him alone. We went on to prayer meeting without him and I told Rae he was under the bed. I was so mad I could have strung him up.

My prayers that evening were so futile that they just seemed to bounce off the ceiling. I was too upset to be in connection with the Spirit of God, let alone the Spirit of mercy. When we got home he was in his room sitting alone in the dark. He said Grandma called, but I knew he called her to try to get her on his side and tell me not to punish him. That infuriated me more, but I called her anyway. Well, she did exactly what I expected of her; she told me the same thing that the pastor was teaching about, the mercy of God.

The pastor was teaching on Jonah; how he finally preached to the Ninevites, but did not want Israel's enemies to receive mercy, for he knew God desires mercy, not punishment. Even though we deserve punishment, God gives us mercy and he who shows mercy shall obtain mercy. I was furious because of his troublesome spirit, his manipulations and disobedience and just think, he ratted to my mother! I told Rae what my mother said and she agreed that I needed to show mercy. I could not believe it! Even my wife was on his side, but as I thought about it I started to calm down. It just struck me how merciful God's Spirit is and how I have frustrated Him time and time again.

Needless to say, I did not spank him, though I did talk to him about all the trouble he kept getting into. I gave him a lesser punishment than what he deserved. I know now that this was God intervening on his and my behalf because I would had spanked him out of anger, not being like God the Father, and we would not had learned about mercy.

Now let's put this in perspective. There are times when fathers need to chasten their children; disciplining them to refrain from bad behavior, not because we are angry with them for what they have done. However, we need mercy to look past the symptoms and see the pathway for healing the problem. Mercy gives us a chance to get it right the next time, and it keeps us from totally destroying the person that needs it. **God, who is rich in mercy, gives it because of his great love for us** (Ephesians 2:4-5). Jesus' love paved the pathway toward a new life for us. Disciplining with mercy reminds our child that we love them in their failures and love for them to grab the opportunity to change so they will not fail again.

The next trait is forgiveness. Have you ever needed your child to forgive you for overreacting to a situation? Yes? Well so have I. I cannot count how many times I read more into something than I should have. I am reminded of the question Peter asked Jesus, **"Lord, how oft shall my brother sin against me, and I forgive him? Till seven times?" And Jesus said unto him, "I say not unto thee, until seven times: but, until seventy times seven"** (Matthew 18:21-22). Fathers, your attitude of forgiveness needs to be as strong as your cry for forgiveness. How many times do you want to be forgiven? Then, you should forgive that many times.

Sometimes fathers hold things over their child's head, such as a dropped pass, a missed shot, striking out with the winning run on third, a failed grade, bad choice of friends, bad decisions in life or an abusive relationship. How about your son's inability to get a job? There could be many reasons, and sometimes fathers seem reluctant to forgive when it crosses their line of rules or opinions. We come up with the unpardonable sin, i.e. our daughter getting pregnant while a teenager, or our son not being the valedictorian or the sport star. We forget how we were, when perhaps we were that type of young man that had the potential to get a young lady pregnant.

The Lord showed me my attitude with my sons.

Who Am I and Where Am I Going From Here?

In some ways, we fathers are harder on our sons. My two sons confronted me when they were teenagers because they had always seemed to be on restriction; they wanted to know why I had a different attitude toward them. I treated them unfairly, they thought, thinking I expected more from them than their sisters. I told them they made excuses to blame others for their behavior and did not use wisdom to stay out of harm's way.

But after thinking about it, I admit there was some truth to it. I did expect my sons to be gentlemen; to be leaders in every area of life, which are good expectations, but I also expected them to be perfect and to be tough, not weak or whiny. I allowed the girls to be less than perfect in some ways and to be weaker vessels. Each gender is different and our approach must be different, but we cannot be sympathetic. We hurt our children if we treat each one the same, or if we feel sorry for them, or if we expect them to be perfect.

My sons were different too, but I categorized them together and I put my daughters in a different category. I learned my oldest son is able to take things better as he was a little tougher. He loves electronics and gadgets. My youngest son is more charismatic, sensitive, and has a smile and personality that draws people and often expresses it in his clothing. Now they both love their family, but they show it differently. It took me some time to learn this about my sons because I was trying to get the oldest to be more sociable and the youngest to be tougher. I had to release them and let them be shaped to their personality (the good part of it).

Daddy, the Trainer

There were, however, standards that I would not lower. They needed to learn to be leaders, get good grades (the best they could), respect girls and women, be involved in church activities and to learn from their bad decisions. God realized what was bound up in the hearts of fathers, for he said, "**Fathers do not provoke your children to anger, lest they be discouraged**" (Colossians 3:21). The world shapes men to be competitors, (physical) fighters, and go-getters. If you want something, you are to go after it no matter who has it or who is in the way. God shapes us to find our manhood in Him first and to be prayer warriors, believing it is Him that will make room for us. He requires men to show acceptance, mercy, compassion and forgiveness, and to do it with godliness and meekness.

These two styles are contrasting and conflicting. When fathers do not have a heart to forgive, nor an attitude of forgiveness, it places a child in a precarious position. They will repeat what they learn and digest the same spirit toward others. Sons will be harsh on their sons and the cycle will go on and on. Do you want to stop the cycle? Do you want your child to have godly character? Ask God to change your heart.

When it comes to punishment, it needs to fit the crime. God is just. Our response needs to be an action rather than a reaction. The action of a punishment after the wrong deed gives the child room to make corrections and grow from discipline; it keeps personal feelings out of it and helps the child to see their part instead of your behavior. To react is like an impulsive move; you have done something and now I have to do something I was not prepared for. So, do not make the punishment too harsh or too soft.

I always responded harshly immediately in my mind, and sometimes it came out of my lips; then I would get it right. I had to learn that fatherhood calls for constant discipline and discipleship. Based on the book of Proverbs, the son is to be disciplined by his father's teaching. I thought a disciplinarian was someone mean and strict until God opened my mind to see it is shaping one's life to overcome obstacles.

My siblings used to say I was like my father because he was a disciplinarian. I did not like that, but I realized that he was helping us to live with character. My children did not always believe I gave the appropriate punishment. Actually, they believed it one percent of the time and sometimes they thought it was inappropriate to the crime they committed. However, I was like my father, I wanted them to use wisdom and would not look past their behavior. Do not treat a step-child like a step-child, or they will resent you. People outside your home should not be able to point out "your" children from your spouse's children. Impartiality with love is the key. **"My brethren, have not the faith of our Lord Jesus Christ, the Lord of glory, with respect of persons"** (James 2:1) God is not a respecter of persons; he executes judgment and love.

He is always ready to forgive and release people from their sins. In my mind was a willingness to evaluate myself. "Am I being too hard or unfair to my natural, step- or adoptive children?" In my heart, I would say, "God, help me to love them as you love me." "Would I give this restriction or punishment to my natural children?" Also know to use age appropriate punishment; do not try to reason with a small child, give them directives.

> **Deuteronomy 10: 17-18**
>
> For the LORD your God is God of gods and Lord of lords, a great God, a mighty, and a terrible, which regards not persons, nor takes reward: He does execute the judgment of the fatherless and widow, and loves the stranger, in giving him food and raiment.

Communication is essential; listen to your spouse. Talk to your children, and most of all, listen to the Holy Spirit. Your spouse may see some things you are doing that you may not realize you are doing. Prepare yourself to hear criticism. Gauge your child's reactions to you and to discipline. Some children may try to manipulate and con you with guilt trips, especially the step-parent, so beware. Natural parents, be honest about your child's behavior and attitude. Do not ever close your eyes to their faults. Interact with your mate in disciplinary actions. Fathers, you may have the last word, but base your decision on the big picture, not on just *your* words.

I remember when Rae and I were first married and this was our blended family's first Christmas together. Rae bought some porcelain dolls. She picked them out, and they matched the personalities of three of our younger girls. I interfered, feeling the second youngest was more mature than the youngest one. I persisted to give her doll to the youngest one. The second youngest is my step-daughter; the youngest is my natural daughter. The youngest girl pouted when she felt she got the bad part; the other girl had a quiet spirit, she did not say anything, but she wore it on her face.

Well, the change was made, and Rae was upset because I was not being honest about my daughter's attitude. I was not fair. My love for my step-daughter was overshadowed by my fear of my natural daughter's response. They both accepted their dolls, but later I found out that they had switched dolls. Actually, my natural daughter accepted the doll that I did not think she would, and my stepdaughter liked the one that she was supposed to have in the first place. Rae was moved by the Spirit, and got the right one for the right children. I should have listened to her. That was the last time I did that, and I apologized to Rae, and our two daughters, and also to God.

So be just, fair, impartial, and share your life equally with all members.

How do you evaluate your actions to your children? How about with your spouse? Are you or your spouse in unity with disciplining the children?

Do I challenge my children, invoking a response or a reaction? Are my training methods adaptable to my family's skills?

Where will my children be in 10 years, after they are released full time into the world?

Who Am I and Where Am I Going From Here?

THE LEWIS FAMILY

James and Rae

Daddy, the Trainer

James, Rae (top),
Shanita, Quan, Joey (center),
Krystal, Jamie and Rachel (bottom).

Jamie, Krystal (left), James, Rae (center left), Quan, Shanita, (Back right) and Rachel (front right)

REDICK FAMILY
Quan, Danielle and Aniya

KENDRICK FAMILY
Clockwise– Rion, Alvin, Marques Jr., Ausia and Shanita

Row 1: Krystal, Grandma Haynes w/Aniya, Jamie w/Grace
Row 2: DeAndre, Michael-Vincent, Rachel, Dario
Row 3: Tarah, Quan Danielle w/Jayshawn, Joey

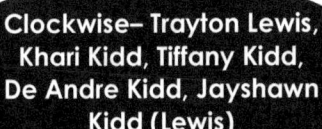

Clockwise– Trayton Lewis, Khari Kidd, Tiffany Kidd, De Andre Kidd, Jayshawn Kidd (Lewis)

Who Am I and Where Am I Going From Here?

Alex and Krystal Wadlington

Kingston and Pierce Wadlington

Daddy, the Trainer

Rachel Lewis and Gabriel Russell

Rachel Lewis and Gabriel Russell

Jamie Lewis

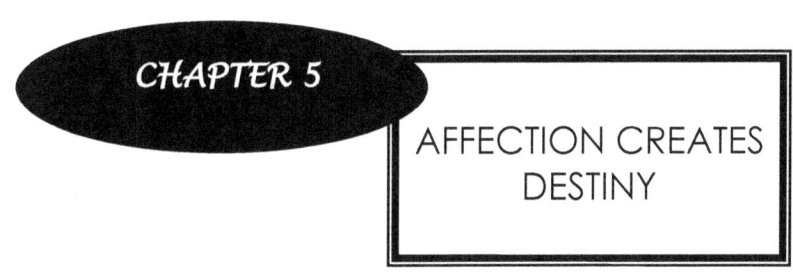

AFFECTION CREATES DESTINY

Last, but not least, be affectionate! Have kind words, playful words, and teasing words (with love). Give hugs and kisses. These are a child's friend and a parent's tool to let children know you accept them. **"Be kind one to another, tenderhearted, forgiving one another, even as God for Christ's sake has forgiven you"** (Ephesians 4:32).

One thing I like to do is tease and play. It helps me to break through walls of communication. My step-son and step-daughter were serious children. Before I came along, they seemed to not have experienced many jokes being cracked or playful times. And when I first started teasing them, they did not know how to take it. One time, early in our relationship, I got my step-son pretty good for something he had done and he was not too happy with me after being lectured. So I started teasing him to let him know it was not personal; we were still "tight". He had had enough of me. He did not want to play, so I tackled him right in the living room and started wrestling and tickling him. After the shock, he loosened up and began laughing and tickling me back. Then our youngest son jumped on us and we all rolled around together while Rae screamed for us to stop. It was fun!

You see, I wrestled with my children all of the time before, especially with my son. The girls were not

Who Am I and Where Am I Going From Here?

excluded, even when they became teenagers and thought they were too cute. I did have to be careful, for there was new growth in some areas. They did need a father's affection without an inappropriate touch so they would know what it is like. This will help them to not be confused about a boy's seductive touch. I even wrestled Rae; she was not much fun though since she would not tickle me back!

My youngest son and I spent a lot of time together. When I remarried, he seemed to resent having a brother and sharing time with me. He was ten years old, and my newest son was thirteen. I had two problems: one was the one mentioned above and the other was that my new son seemed to resent that a man was in his house with his mom. He was the man and now here I was, taking over and bringing in all these children. So my wrestling was a way of physically spending time with both sons. It helped to break down a wall of resentment.

Sometimes the younger girls would pile on, but I had to grab the oldest daughter to get her to play. She was twelve and into herself. She was "too mature for this childish behavior," but she loved it. My new daughter loved the fact that she had a father in the home and new sisters so she changed her last name when her mother changed hers. We let her do it on her papers at school and other unofficial documents.

Now, let's go back to our behavior with preteen (10-12 year old) daughters. I know I realized I had to be careful with my affection, but I could not treat them with a "no-touch" attitude. This is a very important time. You may be unsure about hugging your child or allowing her to sit in your lap like she once did. But find a way to show appropriate affection because she needs to learn how to receive the affection of the opposite sex. Your step- or adopted daughter may not have had a father in their life to receive affection from. My suggestion is be careful; learn your child's ways and communicate with your spouse.

> *Thank the Lord Jesus for direction and refuge!*

My new daughter was very affectionate, however at first, she was hesitant, and Rae was hesitant also, so I waited. She was seven years of age when I married her mother. As she watched the other girl's affection towards me, she felt more comfortable. She is 29 now and would come up and put her head on my shoulder. My oldest daughter and I had the most strenuous relationship out of all the girls. I did not show her more affection than chastisement. I was a dad trying to find direction in my life when I came into her and my first wife's lives. At that time, she was only two years old. After the divorce, she came to know that I was not her real father and she was not with her mother, but with me, her adoptive stepfather. The atmosphere was tense because she was hurt and I was too from the divorce. Thank the Lord Jesus for direction and refuge!

She eventually went to live with her biological mother at 16 and I was not too happy with that decision for many reasons. One, it put a bigger strain on our relationship by the miles, attitudes and lifestyles. I believe those years were lost for me as a father and in many ways my hands were tied because she wanted to get to know her real father and mother. She got pregnant at nineteen, had a son Marques Jr., and she lived with her son's father for a time and was confused about her future. But God, who is rich in mercy and forgiveness, as He had forgiven me for the same actions, had me forgive her and He brought her back to the Kansas City area and gave her salvation. I am proud of her. She has a degree and is married to a loving husband and was three wonderful children.

As for the other girls who had some questionable boyfriends, we were able to communicate through the tough times. There were times of disagreement, though I feel we were able to overcome them by the blood of Jesus, our faith in Him and our testimony on how to be affectionate. This helped me with coaching them in basketball and keeping an appropriate stance with the other young ladies on my team. I kept a father's attitude with them; being concerned about their need for a father's touch, without inappropriateness, as some did not have their father around. One of the young ladies from my summer team came and lived with us. She still has a special place in our hearts as we helped her through college. Later, she went to live with her father and grandparents.

I am a family man, and my children loved family time even as teenagers. They were not ever ashamed that I was their father. Well, at least they did not show it! Family time helps children identify with their past to move toward their future. Both of our parents took us as children on family vacations. This helped our children and they were more than ready to accept and hug their step-parents. Our children found

So we pronounced God's truth over our children to take them from captivity even when they left home

acceptance in who they were and this helped them show us how to hug them even when times were hard.

    I learned that rules without relationships produced rebellion. However, relationships with rules produced righteousness. Family time produces relationships beyond the rules; it was a time of love that covers or overlooks problems. So when our youngest son got into trouble with the law, we needed hugs to get us through the tough times. He still hugs me now when he greets me and when we depart. They are manly hugs; a soul shake with our forearms between each other and then our left arms around each other and embrace. What an experience, to be affectionate and kind to each other, keeping your manhood for God the Father who says in Isaiah 49:15, **"Can a woman forget her sucking child, that she should not have compassion on the son of her womb? Yea, they may forget, yet will I not forget thee." He would also never leave us nor forsake us** (Hebrews 13:5). He is the one who created us to be men and He shows us how to be tender warriors.

    Rae and I would anoint our children with oil, as stated in the Bible, and pray individually for each one first by telling them how appreciative we are to God for them and what we see God is doing in their lives, pronouncing prosperity and blessings from God over their present and future. We also would sit down with each one and let them know we expect what God's expectations were. We wanted them to give God the chance to reveal His purpose and design of who He created them to be and give them the direction they are to go.

Who Am I and Where Am I Going From Here?

God's people of Israel were in captivity, as stated in Jeremiah 29:11-14. The verse says:

Jeremiah 29:11-14

For I know the thoughts that I think toward you, saith the Lord, thoughts of good and not of evil, to give you an .expected end. Then shall you call upon me, and you shall go and pray unto me, and I will hearken unto you. And you shall seek me and find me, when you shall search for me with all your heart. And I will be found of you, saith the Lord; and I will turn away your captivity and I will gather you from all the .nations, and from all your places where I have driven you, saith the Lord; and I will bring you again into this place where I caused you to be carried away captive.

I know this was for Israel, but when God became our Father through salvation, all spiritual blessings that are received through faith in Him, we are made one with the commonwealth of Israel. Read Ephesians 2:1-18.

So we pronounced God's truth over our children to take them from captivity even when they left home. I can still see God working on them now bringing them to an expected end. Speak what God says your child will be and be patient for them to listen to God's word.

Affection Creates Destiny

Are you creating an atmosphere where your children are destined to succeed?

Who Am I and Where Am I Going From Here?

Do you have rules without a relationship that produces rebellion or relationship with rules that produce righteousness?

Affection Creates Destiny

How do you and your family express affection for God, one another and others outside of the home?

_____
_____
_____
_____
_____
_____
_____
_____
_____
_____
_____
_____

CHAPTER 6

FATHERHOOD: A PRIESTLY SERVANT

Jesus says in Mark 9:35, **"If any man desire to be first, the same shall be last of all and servant of all."** The world does not think like that; they say the greatest is the one who rules or dominates everyone else. A lot of us men have that worldly view; we feel we are the kings of our castle and should dominate others. We also strive for position to find identity and power.

When our children were younger and smaller, I could intimidate them with hollering or angry looks, but now that all of the children are twenty-seven years or older, my intimidation days are over. The intimidation factor I am referring to is using our position to make them do the right thing.

When they got older I had to realize that my position does not have much weight unless I am showing service to them and their mother. One day when we were visiting our youngest son – who was living with the mother of his new born boy - we took them some diapers and money. He and I got into a discussion about his work. He felt I was putting pressure on him and he got defensive. He then got very disrespectful to me and raised his voice like he wanted to fight me. One of my pet peeves is a disrespectful child. Years ago I saw a father and son fighting because the son was angry at him for not being there for him and his mother. So I told myself that if any of my children got that angry, I would not fight them because it is a no-win situation.

Well, my blood level rose 400 degrees. But no matter how many times I told him I am your dad and I will whoop your tail, he was not that small child anymore; he was as tall as me. He was defying my position because he felt I did not serve him. The old way of our father-son relationship rose up in me. You see this was how I would intimidate him to do what I felt was right, but now that he was in his twenties he was feeling like he was grown enough to take me on. So I backed off, said it was time for us to leave and we left.

The Spirit of the Lord gave me humility to drop my pride and later he did apologize. We then talked about the situation and got an understanding. If I would have risen up in pride, things would have gotten worse. God was teaching me about the Father's love when the prodigal son wanted to take his inheritance and waste it. A godly father continues to love the child's created potential and not their present circumstance. Our position as a father is an honorable one, however, it is not to put pressure on our children to demand respect.

My son is one of my adoptive children; he did not feel I loved him at times because I reacted to his behavior instead of responding to his being. Fathers, be wise in the choices you make, for they shape the potential of your children. Parenthood does demand children to show respect; honor and obey the position since God says so in Exodus 20:12: **"Honor thy father and thy mother: that thy days may be long upon the**

Fatherhood: A Priestly Servant

land which the LORD thy God gives thee." Matthew 15:4 also says, **"For God commanded, saying, Honor thy father and mother; and he that curses father or mother, let him die the death."** Ephesians 6:1-3 goes on to say, **"Children, obey your parents in the Lord: for this is right. Honor thy father and mother; which is the first commandment with promise; that it may be well with thee, and thou mayest live long on the earth."** And lastly Colossians 3:20 says, **"Children, obey your parents in all things: for this is well pleasing unto the Lord."** However, in Ephesians and Colossians, the next verse after telling the children to obey, it deals with the father's ability to provoke their children to wrath. Showing them service like Christ talks about in Matthew 20:28: **"Even as the Son of man came not to be ministered unto, but to minister, and to give His life a ransom for many,"** and also in Luke 22:27: **For whether is greater, he that sitteth at meat, or he that serveth? Is not he that sitteth at meat? But I am among you as one that serveth."** Service will help you get better results.

He did not say do this because I am the Creator of Heaven and Earth, but because the servant is as his master and the disciple as his Lord. Jesus came to serve and not to be served. My son was under pressure; he just had a son out of wedlock, his finances were not stable, and as a matter of fact, I later found out that he no longer had a job. He was laid off at the time we were there, and he was living with a girl, going against everything we had taught him. He also was going against what God had purposed for him and when we are not in the center of God's will, we feel guilty and do not realize where the guilt is from. For me, to serve him was to listen to his pain and look past his anger.

Since men are usually task-oriented and competitive people by nature, we approach problems with an attitude to conquer and win. We need to feel out our children and the situation; be quick to listen, slow to speak and slow to anger. Stubborn, or strong-willed, children pose a big problem for fathers who want immediate obedience from their children. There are questions that appear disrespectful but the intent is to gain an understanding. As a priestly servant like Christ, the whole idea of discipline is to keep the child functional, while getting rid of the sin. We are to help them focus on Christ and make wise decisions for the future.

There is an attitude of humanism that has swept our land, which is not to physically discipline our child by spanking them. We think it teaches the child violence and damages their psyche. It never damaged mine, nor people that I grew up with or the ones who came up with this thought. It may be politically correct, but it is not biblically correct. In Proverbs 22:15 it reads, **"Foolishness is bound in the heart of a child; but the rod of correction shall drive it far from him."** Earlier, in verse 6, it says, **"Train up a child in the way he should go; and when he is old, he will not depart from it."**

To correct is to discipline and to discipline is to appoint disciples, learners, achievers and leaders. They need to be corrected to learn the direction of success for them. Since each person is different and has a certain talent to present in the family, specific discipline will help direct them toward their success. They may stray from that successful path, but if fathers serve with training and discipline, the child will be put back on track to finish their course. A priestly servant gives wisdom to their children like our heavenly Father does.

    The public does not trust in God the Father and they think they are smarter than Him and as a result, we have schools overrun with youngsters who talk back to teachers, fight each other, are deviant to authority and dropping out without proper training. I could go on and on. Foolishness is pent up actually in the hearts of adults who think they know how to raise children without shaping their character. Fathers, keep this principle in mind; the ones who despise the chastening of their fathers have a deviant heart. They are the same ones that want to change the way character and discipline is to be dealt with. They do not want God to judge their evil hearts so they would have to change. The principle to strengthen children is to put pressure and weight on their character. If they faint in times of adversity, their strength is small. If they make mistakes, love corrects.

    Read I Samuel 2:11 to I Samuel 4:22. Eli the priest had two sons who did not know the LORD and they were taking the people's goods (offerings) and having sex with the women in the temple. God warned him to discipline his sons, but all he did was talk to them and not physically correct them, so God did. Eli was to remove them from their position of authority, but he chose to do it his way, which caused the nation to fall short of their potential. Eli and his sons were to stand as representatives for God and intercessors for a sinful and faulty people.

    The priest is someone who *"stands in the place of," either as a representative or a mediator*. In the Old Testament the priest came from the tribe of Levi, whose name means *"He has enjoined Himself to me"* (Genesis 29:34). Levi was the third child of Jacob (Israel). Both Moses and Aaron were Levites. Their father was Amram, son of Kohath, son of Levi. Their mother was also a Levite (Exodus 6:16-20). Moses grew up as an adopted son of Pharoah, King of Egypt. He was in a blended family until the time for his unveiling to his Hebrew brethren. He came to know he was a priest and a deliverer after he chose to serve his God and his people. His decision to suffer in service gave him direction. Jesus was a step-son to Joseph and a half-brother in His family. He also grew up in a blended family. He knew who He was, though, without having to discover Himself. He was the greatest man and priest to ever live. He created time and changed time.

To get back to Moses, God had a plan to join Israel to Himself through the delivering power of His Word, channeled through Moses. After Moses left Egypt, running for his life for killing a man, God called him back as a representative of God to the children of Israel and to Pharoah. He also stood as a mediator between God and Israel, giving them God's words and interceding for them when they sinned. God told him he could not make atonement or be a sacrifice for Israel because He already has someone for that, Himself. Moses had a position to stay in the presence of God, pleasing Him and serving man. Fathers are the priests in their homes.

First, we serve as the spiritual leader, second, as the head of the home, and third, to stand between God and our children. Job 1:4-5 says:

Fatherhood: A Priestly Servant

Job 1:4-5

> And his sons went and feasted in their houses, everyone his day; and sent and called for their three sisters to eat and to drink with them. And it was so, when the days of their feasting were gone about, that Job sent and sanctified them, and rose up early in the morning and offered burnt offerings according to the number of them all: And Job said, it may be that my sons have sinned and cursed God in their hearts. Thus did Job continually.

Job prayed for his children just in case they sinned. And fourth, fathers you are to give up your old life to start a new one.

Let us look at the role of a spiritual leader in the home. There is a myth that the women are to be more spiritual than the men. There is some truth to it because many men are at home watching sports or sleeping while their wives are at church services, tapping into the presence of God. However, in God's scheme of order, He sets a man as head of the woman, the patriarch, leading the way for the others to follow. Even when Jesus changed water into wine, Mary was under subjection to His word. She said to do whatever He says to do. When His natural father Joseph died, His role as the spiritual leader of the home and His calling as the spiritual guide for all mankind, intensified. He was no longer her son in respect to being under authority to her word, but now He's authorized to do a higher calling. Children view God how they view their fathers. Some people are afraid to approach their dads and likewise are afraid to approach God. If their dad was strict or abusive, then they tend to view God like that. It is an unfair assessment of God, but many people think He is out to punish them. But God's love is so overwhelming and innovative, He loves us and changes our thinking about Him, and then we can change our thinking about our dads. Fathers, this tells me to be approachable. Our children need to know we are loving, innovators and approachable too. We can make something happen in their lives.

And another thing. Do not act out of drunkenness or being high. God says, know what His will is and do not be drunk with wine, which is debauchery, but be filled with the Spirit. He knows alcohol controls emotions and slows the reflexes; it befriends a person then makes them look stupid. Drugs will do the same thing, and it will take your money. Alcohol is the number one destroyer of families, not child abuse. Usually when children are abused, alcohol is involved. A spanking is not abuse, it is discipline. Anything could become abusive when done to the extreme or not properly done. I received many spankings and did not turn out abusive. It shaped my behavior for future success.

One day, a mother went to the grocery store with her children. One of her boys decided to act out when he could not get his way, so she responded with "Mr. Brown" (the belt) and started spanking him. A store clerk saw it and told the store policeman. The cop ordered the woman to stop or he would arrest her for abuse. She said either you let me spank him now, or you (society) will spank him later and pay out money to lock him up. Then the policeman said, "go ahead". We have a group of youth whose parents have neglected them by not disciplining them properly. The parents are listening to society too much.

The book of Proverbs is the number one child development and parental guide, in my opinion. It gives the parent and child godly wisdom, understanding, knowledge, discretion and instruction. It has very sound information for teenagers, helping them to stay away from people who do not have their best interests in mind. It also safeguards against traps and explains the consequences of good and bad choices.

When I was younger I did not know Proverbs was so relevant to the times until I actually applied it. I will give you several examples. Let us say your son is easily influenced or is pressured by gang-bangers. Read Proverbs 1: 10-19.

Proverbs 1: 10-19

> "My son, if sinners entice thee, consent them not. If they say, come with us, let us lay wait for blood, let us lurk (hide) privily for the innocent without a cause... My son, walk not in the way with them... So are the ways of everyone who is greedy for gain; which take away the life of the owners."

Who Am I and Where Am I Going From Here?

Or say your son or daughter needs wisdom concerning proper relationships with the opposite sex, read Proverbs 7:6-27. I am not going to go into this one but read the scriptures and challenge your children.

A priest focuses on how to make their family a great unit. Discipline is to be enforced with preventive as well as corrective measures. It is not just having to deal with rebellion, stubbornness or foolishness. Do not wait until you are angry to do something. Respond with principles to shape their behavior. Never threaten your children; it should be a promise letting your "yea be yea and your nay be nay". Do not break a promise unless it is a wrong situational promise. Every child is born bent toward sin or wrong doing. For this reason, you must never reason with your child when it comes to discipline. They may think their corrections are negotiable and usually they will reason for the lesser discipline.

A priest in the Old Testament spoke for God, establishing His ways in our every day affairs. The father establishes God's ways in the home, being always alert to help his children grow strong spiritually, emotionally, and physically. Too many times we get a word from the street corner where the philosophers hang out, or television and newspapers where issues are solved in 30 to 60 minutes. Sometimes there is not even a solution to the problem that has been presented. These are not places where a priest finds his answers to approach family and individual issues. A priestly servant focuses on what their master will say on particular issues. Books that include these topics are Leviticus, Deuteronomy, and the Gospels.

Fatherhood: A Priestly Servant

When your child does something wrong that causes a break up in the home or they are in so much trouble that they do not know their end from their beginning, as the priest, be prepared to view the situation through God's eyes. Determine the remedy and continue to apply it day after day, week after week until your child is healed. Get some help with the application of the remedy from your mate. Then offer unto God thanksgiving and praise with your child present. The priest is to take the sacrifice from the person giving it to the Lord so the person and the family may progress.

When the child gets to be eighteen or older and they think they are suddenly responsible, there may be a time when they mess up. When this does happen do not be quick to kick them out. Do not be reactive, be proactive. I recall in my early fatherhood years where I thought when my children graduated from high school it was time for them to leave the nest, especially if they were not going to follow the rules. Then a brother in the Lord told me that is not true, it will not be so cut and dry. Well he was right; most of our children were still our dependents after eighteen. I realize that children are never too old for guidance, help and support. Even I still need it. Read Job's example:

Job 1:4-5

> And his sons went and feasted in their houses, everyone his day; and sent and called for their three sisters to eat and to drink with them. And it was so, when the days of their feasting were gone about, that Job sent and sanctified them, and rose up early in the morning and offered burnt offerings according to the number of them all: And Job said, it may be that my sons have sinned and cursed God in their hearts. Thus did Job continually.

Job interceded for his children daily, even when they had their own house.

This is our role; sacrificing our egos, pride, standards, opinions or even our self-righteousness to pray and uphold them. Mothers have an emotional string to their children since they carried them for nine months and bore the pain to bring them into this world. So as fathers, we need to establish a specific area of connection with each child to bind our lives to their concerns emotionally. This connection will allow us to have compassion for our children in the hard times. Sports and music have been good building tools for me but each father has to find his own. This establishes the child's identity and what they contribute to the family.

We have had four of my children move back into the house and two have actually moved out without going to college. By the time our son and daughter moved back in, it was different. My wife and I were faced with a different challenge; my children had become young adults. My daughter was a single mom with a son and my son was married with a daughter, and of course his wife came along with the deal. This was more challenging because we had differences in our lifestyles. We had to pray more and rely on the power of the Holy Spirit of God to keep us focused on the standards we abide by in the home. My challenge was to be supportive, firm and communicative without demands. God never threatens to kick us out of His family when we are not living up to His standards and He expected me to follow His example.

Fatherhood: A Priestly Servant

I remember letting my children know when they were teenagers if they knew everything there was to know, that the door was open for them to leave, but this time things were different. There were still rules to follow and they knew what those were, and they seemed more mature and willing to do it without threats, which made it easier. But there were those times where we did not agree. In the past, we would come to an impasse and I would make them do the right thing, however now I would have to allow them time to decide without pressure. Being the head of the household I had the last word, but I had to understand my son was the head of his household and my daughter was the head of hers since she had a son. What type of example would I be?

They both needed to be respected, and especially my son because he was being trained to be in charge and I could not put him down in front of his wife. I remember my son coming to me to tell me I changed. What he saw before was a father that took the stern, firm approach on rules and now I was longsuffering, allowing time for them to grow. I did not think I changed; I thought I just had a different situation. But after thinking about it I could see the change. The difference was that now I conferred with my wife and we took it to the Lord, and in return He gave them the answer to do what was right.

Even the decision for them to move back was not mine alone. Our children went to their mom first and she brought it to me. Then we sat down to discuss the issues and concerns. We prayed before meeting with them and had prayer when we met, then we let the Lord direct our path, since He is the one with the plan. I saw it as a second chance to get closer to them and to get to know my daughter-in-law and my grandchildren. One Sunday, my daughter decided it was time to surrender her life to Jesus. She got up in front of the church and told them she thought she knew what she was doing, but she messed up her life by not listening to her parents. Now she wanted the Lord to direct her path. My wife and I were in tears. Nine months after my son's return, he decided to turn his life over to God also. You see, God had a plan and we just needed to listen. He knows the direction we are to take, for He has an expected end.

    Now, I know that every situation is different. Comparisons can only be made to hold up a principle, not the method. So when the children who never left were going through crazy times, the principle remained the same. And as a result, I became a wiser dad. Also when other people came to live with us, the principles remained the same. We considered them as our children and asked the Lord to blend us together to show them His purpose for their lives.

    My pride and opinions dissipated the more I talked and listened to God and my wife. I also saw the children mature. In a blended home, show your step- and biological children that you love them; allow them to learn hard lessons while at home. I recall when my children had troubles with the opposite sex and they were not ready to listen. I was upset and did not want anything to do with them. Godly wisdom prevailed and our relationship is stronger because I let them fail. Sometimes success comes with failures. Troubles produce patience and it gives experience, which produces hope. And hope is not ashamed because love is planted in our hearts until our hope is manifested:

> **Romans 5:3-5**
>
> And not only so, but we glory in tribulations also: knowing that tribulation worketh patience; And patience, experience; and experience, hope: And hope maketh not ashamed; because the love of God is shed abroad in our hearts by the Holy Ghost which is given unto us.

In a blended home, never treat anyone like their title: step, half, or adoptive. Treat them as you would want to be treated by your parents; as a son or daughter who wants to receive their full inheritance for being yours.

Servanthood is not a word that will make fathers jump up and down and rejoice. Since we like to be our own person, doing whatever pleases us, for we like to be served. Then when we do serve others it is like a waiter looking for tips and wages for our service. We have a hard time doing it wholeheartedly, totally giving ourselves to someone else. If a husband serves his wife, other men usually call him "henpecked". If the wife serves her husband, the ladies say he is a "dictator" and is oppressing her. If the children serve their parents, then their peers usually call them "losers" unable to make decisions for themselves. If an employee serves their employer, their co-workers say they are "brown-nosing". Our mentality is not to serve, but to be served. We feel it is too costly or too hard. "I just cannot be me" or "I am not free" are statements of "me-ology" which sum up the way we live today. As it is written, Jesus said to all that will be His disciple, **"If any man will come after me, let him deny himself, and take up his cross and follow me"** (Matthew 16:25). Jesus also said, **"Even as the Son of man came not to be ministered unto, but to minister, and to give His life a ransom for many"** (Matthew 20:28).

When I look back at my father's life and how he got together with my mother, committed himself to her and sacrificed for the family's welfare, it showed me how to serve. He was young when he married her with a baby on the way, but no matter what the circumstances were, he pressed through them to stay married for sixty-two years to the same woman. He served her until death parted them on his birthday, September 16, 2005. It seemed like he was more equipped for tough times. Maybe it was his lack of luxuries or the understanding that he was here to bless his children, the next generation. I believe the older generation was taught how to be more responsible and to think about others more at a young age. I even picture my father-in-law and how he also sacrificed for his family of 12. He gave up his life to serve them.

So the question is, "How do we serve our family now?" Well, much should be the same. We should be committed, faithful and always willing to give up what we want. The next question is, "How do I keep my identity as a man if I am a servant?" First, we need to realize we serve someone every day, either ourselves or someone else. For we are created to serve. Either we will serve God, Satan, friends, ourselves, employers or whomever else. For example, if I am hanging out with the guys and the topic comes up of how they treat their wives, and I go home and start treating my wife the same way, then I just served my peers by doing what they thought. Unfortunately, there are people who receive advice from the wrong sources and whenever that person yields their ears and heart to the information, they have become a servant to that thing or person they listened to. I suggest that you read Romans 6-8. God created us to serve Him: **"Thou art worthy, O Lord, to receive glory and honor and power: for thou hast created all things, and for thy pleasure they are and were created"** (Revelation 4:11).

Let us explore more of the first question, which was "How do we serve?" While walking to Jerusalem, James and John went to Jesus asking this question. When He would come into His glory, he would allow them to sit one on the right and one on the left. They wanted the prestigious seats, but Jesus let them know it was not His to give but the Father's. Then He asked them a question, "Can you drink from the same cup He would partake from?" They, of course said yes and He said they would by suffering. My point is on the principle of suffering through serving. Because Jesus next said if you want to be the greatest in the kingdom of heaven, you must be the one who serves all. What a twist to our psyches and egos!

Fathers, the key to serving is first to have a willing spirit to sacrifice for your family in prayer, in reading the Bible and being the example in speech, conduct and work. Prayer and reading the word are like salt on food. It brings out the taste that was hidden and it also preserves the food. Understand that whatever your profession is, it is all for the benefit of others. Your income and abilities are not yours, but the entire family's. Your thinking is a great recompense to your results. And if your wife works, her income is not hers either, but the family's. Think unity! A blended family's worse enemies are miscommunication, disunity and selfishness. Wisdom builds the house and doing it together keeps it going. Your wife needs to know what is yours is hers and hers is yours. This is why you should not have separate bank accounts; it works against your success.

God made the male and female one. Rae and I do everything together, and not just because it works for us. I can hear some of you saying, "That's good for you, but we are different," but the truth is, we do things together because God said to. Jesus said a house divided would not stand, so we literally take His advice to stay together. Our investments and all financial decisions are discussed before we act on them. My beneficiary is, and will be, my wife unless she passes on before me.

Be a servant to your employer and your children will learn from your example. Be sure to prioritize your efforts. I worked in a union at a gas company. My first effort was directed toward the glory of God being seen by co-workers. Then my effort went toward serving my employer and then the union. Why the union last? This is because my Lord saved me and gave me the abilities to do the job, my employer next because they hired me to demonstrate my salvation and my abilities, and then the union because they helped management to keep the contractual agreement. Even though the union negotiates your wages, they do not sign the paychecks.

Fatherhood: A Priestly Servant

In the family you are the employer, you sign the checks for your children. They can negotiate their curfew and other things but you make the decisions. In Luke 3:14; John was talking to the Roman soldiers for them to be content with their wages: **"And the soldiers likewise demanded of him saying, and what shall we do? And he said unto them. Do no violence to no man, neither accuse any falsely; and be content with your wages."** It is hard to do your best when you are underpaid and conditions are lousy, but realize the greater goal is to please your Master, your Creator.

"For where your treasure is, there will your heart be also" (Matthew 6:21). And I say where your heart is, that is where you will direct your efforts, resources and time. How you prioritize your time will show what you are interested in. If your family's existence rotates around you, then you are not a good servant or steward. For example, just say after work you are tired so you go home and plop onto the couch or your favorite chair. You are there until dinnertime, but then you return back to your chair until bedtime. This goes on day after day. Your wife also works, whether it is in the home or outside. After she gets off work she has to cook, help with the children's homework and get them to bed, while you are waiting for her to take care of your needs. Serving your family by working is great, but it is not the only thing to do.

A servant also spends time serving others at home, not being served. It is okay to relax and wind down, but your wife needs to wind down also. Your blended family especially needs you as the leader to be the example of service. This exemplifies your love and acceptance to your old members and new ones. A father should be secure enough to not have to be the center of his family's attention. Giving your time and effort tells them of your heart's purpose. We have six children and other young people that have stayed with us, so we shared responsibilities. Many times I would cook and let Rae relax. When the children were old enough to do work they would have to be accountable to do them.

I would listen to their day, as much as they would let me know, of course. Communication was great when my children were in elementary school, but along came those teenage years and secrecy was a given. I was very persistent in breaking that oath. We had four college students, my son, and his wife and child living with us at one time and we all shared responsibilities. I noticed that my son learned this lesson and he serves his wife by doing dishes, folding clothes and letting her relax.

School activities should be a high priority and should be kept there when your children are involved in them. My children were involved. So even though it felt like we were going every night, it only lasted for a short time. Because there came a time when they left the house, and looking back it did not seem long enough. Just to be present at our children's events showed a lot of love and concern for them. I have seen parents deliberately keep their children out of activities because they said they did not have the time or energy. Maybe you can utilize your neighbors and friends for transportation or other parents on the team; those are good relationship builders. You need to schedule your time with the children. A sometime commitment is better than any sacrifice of not being there! My father came to my games late sometimes because of his work schedule, but I would still look forward to his arrival. I was so excited that he came even if it was late.

Schedule family time for devotions, watch TV together, or turn it off for family discussion or reading. Go do activities together and take vacations together. In our early years, we played softball and basketball together. We find time to visit each other now and then. I believe we are closer as a family because I scheduled my time to serve and be there to watch them sing, play sports or instruments, talk to teachers, and see them get honored for their achievements.

Be involved! There are some dads that are there at the home, but their mind and their heart are elsewhere. Do you remember being in school and the teacher going over the answers that would be on the next test, but you were not paying attention to the answers? So when the test was given out you did not have a clue what to do, so you failed that exam. Even though you were present you were not prepared. Some dads are there but not prepared for the daily test that their children give when they are asking for attention. Their involvement with their family is not enough to warrant their child's belief that they care. Involvement is a big issue in any family structure, but more so in a blended one.

I want you to ask yourself this question, "Who do I want my legacy to be remembered best by, my family or the world?" "We all get 24 hours in a day, so how and where do I spend my time?" "Am I using my time wisely and producing the results to help my family grow?" It is funny how we put in countless hours of work to get things for our family to have that our parents could not afford only for them to reject them or use them for a short time. What they really want is our involvement with them. Money and things are nice to have and they may even be important, but not to the expense of losing your relationship with your family.

In school, studying to pass a test required sacrificing your playtime to get a good grade. Your understanding of the subject matter increased and your parents became proud of how well you did. Young children require high maintenance and teenagers require repair work because everything you teach them becomes broken and you are constantly fixing their behavior. At one time in our household, all six of my children were teenagers at the same time. Life seemed imminent to them but not to us. Our biggest challenge was to know them, how they reacted to situations and how to repair things so that they would not fail again, which did not always work out. At times, our children seemed like aliens to us. We felt we could not trust them to date, drive, come home on time, or to have the right people over because they proved to be untrustworthy. And sometimes they felt they could not trust us, their parents. But then at times, they did show that they could be trusted. So how could we get them to be trustworthy all of the time? Some things take time and a change in their nature had to happen. Trust is earned, respect is given! One thing we did not do was look past their behavior. We held them accountable and disciplined them when they messed up.

I took the lead on this, but I also expected my wife to support me. Mothers, please do not lessen the restriction without consenting with your husband after he disciplines them. It causes too many problems, and it hinders the unity of the parents. Even if he is the stepfather the child will not respect his authority if you do. Also, never tell the child that they are acting like their biological parent (the one that they are not living with). It alienates you from the child creating a barrier like the Berlin Wall. My children were with me when their real mom left and like her, two of them ran away from their problems. I had to keep my mouth closed, which was hard. At times I lectured them too long and made them feel like they would always be irresponsible. But we did not put their other parent down in front of them. We found proper times to discuss their behavior and how it might have been similar to their other parent.

Who Am I and Where Am I Going From Here?

Which direction are you leading your family?

_____
_____
_____
_____
_____
_____
_____
_____
_____
_____
_____
_____

Fatherhood: A Priestly Servant

Is your service to propel your children or step-children into their destination or yourself?

Who Am I and Where Am I Going From Here?

Identify your children's talents and involve yourself in their life. List your children and their talents here.

Are you prioritizing your daily life to have your next generation prioritize theirs?

_____
_____
_____
_____
_____
_____
_____
_____
_____
_____
_____
_____

CHAPTER 7

MOM, THE WARRIOR

When I was young, I could not understand why girls were tattlers and how they could do it so effortlessly and without remorse. I could never imagine myself running to tell on my brothers and friends to the authorities - probably because I was involved in the mischief which would also create a conflict with them and me. Some girls, not all, seem to find their talent in tattling, exciting and rewarding. They appear to enjoy watching their brothers or male classmates squirm while getting into trouble. They seem to discard the pain that the boys could inflict upon them. Girls also seem to be more honest and smarter academically than boys, but actually they are not; they just navigate to what is right more frequently, instead of what is wrong. Criminal activity is not as much of an issue with girls. Plus, they have more of a tendency to fight for the rights of others.

This is what I want you to see—moms that will stand and fight. There are fewer women in prison and fewer girls in gangs. Girls are more likely to support the school activities, graduate from high school and college and get a job. Why? I believe it is because of their nature to follow; they do not want to live in chaos. Women want to be secure. Love stories thrill them, while guys think they are sickening. They thrive on love, and it energizes their emotions.

Even though women are the weaker sex, they are more willing to be strong and take a stand against wrongdoing. They have formed a group called MADD (Mothers against Drunk Drivers). There is also a group called SADD (Students against Drunk Drivers), which is mostly made up of females. Why is not there a FADD for fathers? I don't know. However, mothers also fight more for children. Statistically, there are approximately the same amount of single mothers and fathers, but there are more fatherless homes. More mothers are on the PTA, more mothers fighting against abortion, sexism and more single mothers in the House of God. Mothers are bonded to their child for life; they feel the pain their children go through because they went through a bonding period. When they carried them for nine months they learned their cry, their personality and mood swings. Therefore they are more equipped to fight for the children; mothers live by their emotions and feel by their heart, not their head. Jesus, in Hebrews 4:14-15, feels what we feel and was tempted like us but knew no sin:

Hebrews 4:14-15

> *Seeing then that we have a great high priest, that is passed into the heavens, Jesus the Son of God, let us hold fast our profession. For we have not an high priest which cannot be touched with the feeling of our infirmities; but was in all points tempted like as we are, yet without sin.*

He laid down His life willingly for us and mothers are that way, except for the "no sin" issue. Rae has stood her ground for her step-children even when others thought she should not take on this endeavor. In a blended home, children need time and space to adjust to their step-mom. Draw from your experience of growing up and adjusting to the new schools when you went from elementary to middle school and then to high school.

Even though mothers are more emotional than fathers, they seem to be tougher mentally. More mothers who find themselves without a husband, raise their children despite the hard times, whereas the fathers many times abandon them. As I stated before, there are fathers who persevere through hard times with their families; my father and father-in-law were two of them. I can also name numerous other fathers such as my brothers, uncles, and friends who did not run out on their children or their wives and I applaud them. However, more mothers raise their children without fathers than fathers raising their children without mothers.

The first tactical strategy to the fight is to get into the mind of your step-child by involving yourself in their life. Show you care through establishing achievable expectations for your children. Give them age-level responsibilities and challenges that the children will need your help in. Be a room-mother if your job allows the time. Meet with the teacher regularly, not just during conference time. My natural and adoptive daughters had a teacher in grade school after Rae and I were first married that, to this day, has never noticed that they were not biological siblings. She also constantly talked about how well Rae and I raised them and the involvement we had with the school and the children. Rae had a full time job and she still made sure she kept up with her children's education. More importantly the outsiders, those that were not in the family, could not say she was partial to her natural children and impartial to her step-children.

Take them to the House of God; this is, strategically, the most important fight plan. It teaches them to love Him and serve Him, also to love others and serve others and the first people they learn to serve and love is their family. Even if they are not biologically bonded, they are mentally, purposely and spiritually bonded. Even our church members could not tell whose children were hers and mine. They were ours and we were theirs.

Whatever your children are involved in, involve yourself and involve them in whatever you are involved in. Rae's job had her doing a lot of community service, educating young and old on safety with natural gas, so to keep the family together she involved us. I was McGruff, the crime fighting dog, when she went to the schools and businesses to teach safety. She was also involved in ABWA (American Business Women Association) where we both participated in community service. We also made sure that our children were involved. The more involved you are when they are young, the easier your communication will be and the quicker their adjustment will be. They will realize you have their best interest in mind and later when they grow up, they will have your best interest in mind and also their children's best interest. They will more than likely become more involved with community and church activities when they grow older.

Mom, the Warrior

Each one of our six children has talents that are individually theirs even though some overlap with others. However, the big fight was to make them believe they were more important than our jobs and our personal agendas. Even when we were guardians to several young people that stayed with us, we made sure we involved them. Sometimes our children said we were over involved, but at least we were involved. One young lady who is married now with two children keeps us abreast on their activities because when she stayed with us we made ourselves (especially my wife) available to her. The other young folks who had stayed with us got the same treatment. My wife mothered them also and I can honestly say that in our conversations of their lives, my wife would take their side. My wife, because of her fight for the children, no matter who they were, has received Mother's Day cards and phone calls from them even to this day.

But the greatest fight is a spiritual fight. This attacks the enemy directly and frees the person to be the best they could be. As I stated before, the diverse backgrounds and spiritual tendencies in a blended family carry into the household. If you focus only on the physical behavior and not understand it is the spirit that pushes the person's buttons, you limit your ability to fully help them. Mothers, learn the art of spiritual warfare illustrated in Matthew 12:25-29; 43-45; and II Corinthians 10:3-6. Read those scriptures. The fight is not against people, but against Satan, principalities and evil rulers in dark places. I have seen mothers fight teachers, policemen, judges, lawyers and even pastors because their child was constantly in trouble. Because they believed in their children no matter what, their faith in who they will become was greater than who they were at the time of trouble. However, do not spoil your child by keeping them from what and who can save them.

    First, understand your child's behavior and their heart; is it to do what is right or not? Next help them to understand God and their ability, or lack thereof, to control themselves. But most of all, help them understand their need for dependency on someone. It should first be the parent. Then as they grow and mature, teach them their dependency on the LORD. And since God is a Spirit and the devil is a spirit (a created angel) either your child will be controlled by one or the other. Spiritual warfare is an everyday battle of attacking the motive that influences behavior. It addresses the thought-patterns, analysis of ways, and the why's.

    Proverbs 13:24; 22:8, 15; 23:12-23 and 29:15 are passages that speak of the rod of discipline against foolishness. It will tell you how to apply it and what results you will get. Too many times mothers are afraid or apprehensive to use the rod to drive foolishness out of their children, especially their step-children. Possibly for sympathy reasons, usually the fathers are the disciplinarians. The rod is not just a stick to fan their fanny, but the rod is the Word of God or the Sword of the Spirit (Ephesians 6:17). Use it while directing your children. God's Word changes attitudes and will drive an evil spirit out of people. Do your children have a heart to listen to correction? If so, remember, **"A word fitly spoken [is like] apples of gold in pictures of silver. [As] a earring of gold and an ornament of fine gold, [so is] a wise reprover upon an obedient ear"** (Proverb 25:11-12).

Do I nurture my children in agreement with my husband or their father?

Do I fight people or principalities that affect my love ones?

Do I rescue my children, enabling them or help them grow up through adversities?

CHAPTER 8: MOTHERS: CHRIST'S: MODEL TO THE FAMILY

There is a saying that goes, *"Since God could not be everywhere He made mothers."* Well, we know this is not true since God is omnipresent, or everywhere at the same time. But I would say, since God knew we needed to be nurtured and given a tender touch, He gave us mothers. They tend to be gentler and more compassionate than dads. They also feel the situation and not just see it. Women are emotional beings; they also appear to respond to spiritual things more readily than men. I believe this is the reason why we see more women in church settings than men; they seek the security of love.

God placed His touch on women to be strong enough to carry children for nine months and understanding enough on how to feel for other mothers when they are in that season. Women are excellent midwives because they are more empathetic, whereas men would tend to tell them to suck it up and be strong. Because of sin, women feel pain during the pregnancy and the child birthing process. Because of sin, Jesus bore the pain of His disobedient creatures (mankind). He nurtured the disciples with His Word, giving them daily what they needed to survive. It takes only a touch of grace and power to have your body as a shelter for life to grow, to birth forth the child and then tend to their needs and wants. She sacrifices her own health and lifestyle for the health of her baby. When women refuse to sacrifice in giving up junk foods, cigarettes, liquor or drug use, we usually see the baby have some type of abnormality.

A step- or adoptive mother needs a special dose to deal with someone else's children and developing him or her to be a part of a new family unit while allowing them to be who God created them to be. Humans have a tendency to love their own; Jesus said in Matthew 5:46-48, **"For if you love them which love you, what reward do you have? Do not even the sinners do the same? And if you salute your brethren only, what do you more than others? Do not even the sinners also? Be you therefore perfect, even as your Father which is in heaven is perfect."** This type of mother may not bear the physical marks of birthing forth their step- or adoptive child, but they are living out the emotional marks and mandate to love them like Christ loves all children. In Romans 5:20b-21 it states, **"But where sin abounded, grace did much more abound: That as sin have reigned unto death, even so might grace reign through righteousness unto eternal life by Jesus Christ our Lord."** If the child is more dysfunctional than others, they need more grace.

Rae seemed to be equipped by Christ to apply the grace whenever needed. I remember after about two years into our marriage, one of our girls did not have a clean dress to wear to Sunday school. Rae had a top and skirt that she could fit, but our daughter had a tantrum. She was a teenager and it was not stylish enough for the teenage look. I screamed at her for not being grateful, but Rae understood. She empathized with her concern of wearing clothes that were not in style. Then, she got her to wear them. This was her stepdaughter. She understood that this young girl had to readjust to another mother, more siblings and a different peer group.

I failed to say when I married Rae, I moved from Topeka, Kansas to Grandview, Missouri, which is south of Kansas City. Rae had already been there for a year, but my four children had to find new friends while trying to keep up with the latest trends. Children may form a view of God the Father from seeing their earthly fathers. However, they may look at their mothers and see Jesus Christ, the one who is touched by their weaknesses and will sympathize with them. Even the home is designed to have children learn to live practically by their mother as she is the homemaker. So the same applies with Jesus Christ as He practically showed us an example of how to live godly lives.

Our daughter, even though she's out of the house, calls frequently to talk with her step-mother for advice or just to talk. If you are a mom that is rough, maybe it is because of your past experiences: Read Proverbs 9 and 31 to soften your touch and understand that it is not the child's fault; they just need special care.

I was watching the program "Animal Planet" with my youngest daughter one day when a particular segment came on about female animals. They showed a baby bird that had fallen out of the nest, so to protect it the mother bird faked a broken wing to divert the attention away from her fallen baby to herself. Another piece was about a lioness that sheltered her cubs from hyenas and the male lion. People are not animals or mammals because God made people different, however when there are tragic things that happen, mothers are the first to lead in the battle to protect the children.

In Luke 13:34, Jesus cries out to Jerusalem, the holy city of Israel, **"O Jerusalem, Jerusalem, which killest the prophets and stonest them that are sent unto thee; how often would I have gathered thy children together, as an hen doth gather her brood under her wings and ye would not!"** Jesus longs to gather his children up like a hen, protecting them from the evil one. They were like sheep without a shepherd. Similarly, no matter how much pain a child may cause their mom, she still wants to protect, shelter and rescue them. Fathers say put them out and let them learn, while the mothers say bless them with knowledge and understanding to help them learn.

Wisdom is in the female anointing while faith is the male's. It is active in pleasing the authority and releasing the promises. Wisdom has built her house and hewn out her seven pillars (principles) to give longevity to a family unit. Mothers apply the sanctifying knowledge of life and fathers are the works of faith that ignites performance in the home. The mothers explain the whys and the fathers tell them that they need to do it.

More moms are involved in their child's education, social functions and spiritual welfare. Mothers are leaders in the home, school, church and community. The mother who blends the step-, adoptive and natural children together is a great cook. The siblings need to see that they individually play a special role to a greater gain, the cooperative function of the family.

Mothers: Christ's Model to the Family

There are several challenges for women, which are similar to men. One is how would my new husband treat my children, especially my little girls? I realize there is sexual misconduct in the homes; for mothers, sometimes their concerns come to fruition in their home and it destroys the child and their relationship. In the first year of our marriage, Rae had a dream. She was protecting one of our daughters from me. In the dream I attacked her and our daughter and Rae stood against me. She was willing to fight me even though we were intimate partners and I was bigger and stronger.

Now to rest your minds, the dream never came to reality, thank the Lord! It was one of her fears that never came true. But also remember Satan will do anything to destroy your home. My wife is not a physical fighter by nature. She is a spiritual fighter, but her love for her children will make her protect them physically as a shield. Before you marry the man, check out his faithfulness to the Lord, his relationship to his mother and if he has sisters, pay attention to how he relates to them. Never take anything for granted; look for signs and pray. After marriage, continue to check out their relationships and have faith in God. Remember, you are not in a battle with your husband, but you are in battle with the evil rulers of a perverse and twisted, distorted generation. Rae is a spiritual fighter though, as I mentioned, using the Word of God to fight her battles. It is the Spirit that sustains or destroys, so if you are fighting flesh and blood and not the spiritual, you will lose the battles and eventually the war. If you are a praying wife and mother you will receive your dead back to life, rescuing them from fiery trials and the mouths of lions and seeing the promises God has for your family.

Mothers, many times put their children ahead of their husbands, not all of them, of course. Maybe it is because they feel their husband can fend for themselves, but the child needs him to protect them. I heard one mother-in-law tell her daughter to never put the man over the children. That mother was divorced from the girl's father and the daughter eventually got divorced later on. Bad advice! The husband and wife are one, not the mother and the child. Do not orchestrate division with your authoritative partner. This only causes your children to learn how to split you and their father. Your vow is to your man in front of God and witnesses.

In a blended home, it is easy to choose your child over their step-father because of the bond. Some things that demoralize respect are, "He is not really your father," "He does not understand us like we do," "Honey, do not discipline my children," or "Mister, do not try to take the place of their father." Things to say are, "Whatever your father decides I will follow," "Listen to your father," "Honey, we need to decide what to do about…" or "Why not spend more time with your child to understand them?" The words that you speak make or break your relationships. Words will build up or tear down. So tear down the negative and build up the positive. **"Death and life are in the power of the tongue; and they that love it shall eat the fruit thereof"** (Proverbs 18:21).

Do not make judgment calls on your husband, ex-spouse or about your child's father in front of them; get alone with your husband and with God to voice your thoughts. Many of our judgment calls are emotionally driven, siding with the child. If you have already committed treason against your husband, repent to God and apologize to him and your child. If you suspect a problem with their relationship, be open and honest with him and observe signs of abuse. Do not treat him like an outsider. Your children and his are now "ours". Let go of knowing what is best for them and understand that God knows what is best. Do not compare negatively your son to their father. Strive to edify him and his father. A great compliment to Rae and I are when people say "I cannot tell which child belongs to whom". Even when a teenage girl moved in with us, people thought she was our daughter. Rae also did not constantly run down her ex-spouses in the open.

Another challenge is to trust your new family members. Trust is easy before problems challenge relationships. However, mothers seem to be very trusting and trustworthy people. They have their names changed to their husband's to build a legacy for their family. They entrust their children into systems to advance them to prosper and stand beside the children to fulfill their destiny. Children need to learn to trust others and to be trustworthy. Parents, understand that the children will test your trustworthiness and theirs. Family storms will arise frequently in the beginning as if to say, "you are in boot camp to prove yourself to us, whether you are worthy of our trust."

If you have teenage step-children, then just get yourself ready for many tests and trials. And remember this too will pass. How you handle the storms now determine if you will have a strong relationship with the child in the future. Look at the trials as building blocks to teach trust. Teenagers will break trusts that seem to be their makeup. It is not like they mean to, it is just that they are trying to fit into home and more importantly their peer group, so they seem schizophrenic or double minded.

If you teach them their worth in Jesus while they are experiencing teenage situations, eventually they realize they can build trust that matters in life. So do not get bent out of shape (something my wife says) when they do something out of the ordinary from what you do now. Use it to teach them life issues like dependability, trust and faithfulness. I tend to remember my teenage years; I know my parents thought I was not their child at times by the way I acted, unless they thought about their teenage years. And when you need to respond to their behavior do not react from your past behavior, thinking because you messed up in the past you do not have the authority to correct them. Discipline them according to what is right and if mercy needs to be applied then apply it but always do it with grace, faith and love. Mercy gives them another chance, but grace makes them over comers.

Faith is worked by love to put your children into good hands to help. God's hands are better than *Allstate's* hands. Hold fast to faith to believe they will make it, and love to cover their mistakes and shortcomings while they are trying to make it. Mothers, remember there is still absolute truth residing in good and bad choices. When our children tried to reason their penalties and punishments, Rae reasoned with them in truth to their circumstance. Once again, when I said do not react from your past, I mean do not allow them to continue doing wrong because you have done wrong in the past. Parents seem to dwell on this a lot; I see some parents condoning sin because they think they are only human. There was a woman who gave her teenage daughter birth control pills because she felt her daughter would not be able to control herself since she could not when she was young. Well, you may know what happened next. The girl took it as a license to be sexually active and she ended up pregnant.

When our children were younger than fourteen we would restrict them for a set period of time, but after that we would restrict them until we felt they understood and worked on building trust back. God knows we are human and He knows we are incapable to live righteously without sin and faults, so He gives us the opportunity to receive His son Jesus to cleanse us from sin and give us power to live above our faults. However, God still expects us to abide by His standards and principles. So He gives His Spirit to all who ask Him through His Son. Jesus said in Matthew 7:11, **"If ye then, being evil, know how to give good gifts unto your children: how much more shall your heavenly Father give the Holy Spirit to them that ask Him?"**

Jesus teaches His disciples how to love despite sin. In I Peter 4:8 it reads, **"And above all things have fervent charity among yourselves: for charity shall cover the multitude of sins."** Charity is love in action. When a child breaks trust and never has to earn it back, they learn to be irresponsible and undependable, they cannot be trusted.

Mothers, if you have just remarried within the last two years, be on guard. There are many tests that come with the territory: your response to your husband, children (yours and his), the job and relatives. Those relatives are yours, but they are also his and his children's biological mother and her relatives are yours and your children's biological father and his relatives. Proving yourself as a trustworthy mom is essential in the first two years. Remember when you first started a job, brought your baby home, or met a future friend? Others had to get to know you and learn that you were interested in them or how well you handled things. Well, this is how you prove trustworthiness in marriage and family.

Just as Jesus took the initiative to give the people hope and love in God the Father, you are that mediator for your new family. How you respond to your husband will be an indication of how your children will adjust to the new family. Work hard to build up trust and be trustworthy with money and intimacy. Even if your husband breaks the trust, stay trustworthy. Give him chances to re-build the trust lost; your children are watching to see if they need to give their step-dad another chance. Trust builds character and character builds confidence; a person who can be trusted grows stronger mentally and they feel confident they will succeed. Success proves the person can be trusted.

A biological family, as I stated before, is a team with similar traits and style, but a blended family is a team with contrasting styles that have to learn to trust each other's abilities to achieve unity. Mothers, you need to be a character and confidence builder. God has put something in you as a woman to feel more emotions than the man. As Jesus stood in the gap between man and God, be prepared to stand in the gap mediating between the father and your children. To stand in the gap is to bring together not to split apart.

> **II Corinthians 5:18-19**
>
> And all things are of God, who hath reconciled us to Himself by Jesus Christ and hath given us the ministry of reconciliation; to wit, that God was in Christ, reconciling the world unto Himself, not imputing their trespasses unto them; and hath committed unto us the word of reconciliation

If dads begin to provoke the child, pray for them and gain an understanding of their position. God addressed the provocation issue to fathers not mothers, so obviously He knew women were less likely to be volatile towards their child. So the issue God addresses with young mothers is for them to allow the aged women to teach them how to love their husbands and children, and to be sober-minded and balanced emotionally and spiritually. Do not only be lead by your heart, but by the Word of God. In Titus 2:4-5 it says, **"That [aged women] may teach the young women to be sober, to love their husbands, to love their children. To be discreet, chaste, keepers at home, good, obedient to their own husbands, that the word of God be not blasphemed."**

There are many more challenges facing mothers in a blended home such as quiet time - time spent with your man and the children individually, versus his time with the children. I, of course, suggest you take as much time as allowed to spend with God praying, meditating, reading or just relieving your mind, but spend a night every week alone with your husband to build your togetherness. Suggest to your man to spend time with the children and press the children to be with him. Build up your husband in front of the children. The more time is spent with individuals, the less resentment is felt. Observe any attempt of division that creeps in. Provide purpose, structure, direction and discipline for your home. Jesus said in John 5:19-20:

John 5:19-20

> *Verily, verily, I say unto you, The Son can do nothing of Himself, but what He see the Father do: for whatever things He do, these also the Son likewise. For the Father loves the Son, and shows Him all things that He does: and He will show Him greater works than these that you may marvel.*

Just as Jesus got the vision from the Father, your vision comes from your husband and you give it to your children so that the world may marvel at how well your blended home functions. And if your husband is not spiritually in tune with God through Jesus then pray, fast and sanctify yourself so that he can be. I Corinthians 7:13-14 says:

Mothers: Christ's Model to the Family

I Corinthians 7:13-14

> And the woman which hath an husband that believes not and if he be please to dwell with her, let her not leave him. For the unbelieving husband is sanctified by the wife, and the unbelieving wife is sanctified by the husband; else were your children unclean, but now is holy.

Jesus is the chief cornerstone that holds the family together for a habitation for God through the Spirit. The family is part of the foundation that God fitly frames together to build His Kingdom. So let us blend our hearts together in love and see our next generation go to the heavenly dimension. God bless you!

www.ingramcontent.com/pod-product-compliance
Lightning Source LLC
Chambersburg PA
CBHW051449290426
44109CB00016B/1681